FIRST 50 SONGS
YOU SHOULD FINGERPICK ON THE GUITAR

ISBN 978-1-4950-3117-5

HAL•LEONARD®
CORPORATION
7777 W. BLUEMOUND RD. P.O. BOX 13819 MILWAUKEE, WI 53213

Visit Hal Leonard Online at
www.halleonard.com

RHYTHM TAB LEGEND

Rhythm Tab is a form of notation that adds rhythmic values to the traditional tab staff.

TABLATURE graphically represents the guitar fingerboard. Each horizontal line represents a string, and each number represents a fret. Rhythmic values are shown using ovals, stems, and dots.

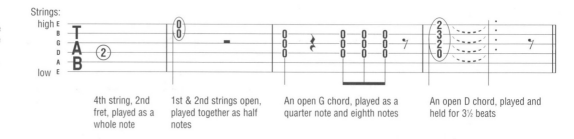

| 4th string, 2nd fret, played as a whole note | 1st & 2nd strings open, played together as half notes | An open G chord, played as a quarter note and eighth notes | An open D chord, played and held for 3½ beats |

Definitions for Special Guitar Notation

HALF-STEP BEND: Strike the note and bend up 1/2 step.

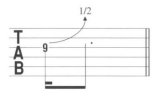

WHOLE-STEP BEND: Strike the note and bend up one step.

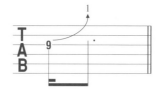

GRACE NOTE BEND: Strike the note and immediately bend up as indicated.

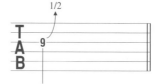

SLIGHT (MICROTONE) BEND: Strike the note and bend up 1/4 step.

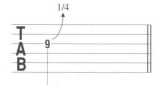

BEND AND RELEASE: Strike the note and bend up as indicated, then release back to the original note. Only the first note is struck.

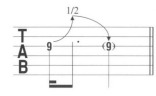

PRE-BEND: Bend the note as indicated, then strike it.

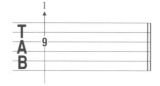

PRE-BEND AND RELEASE: Bend the note as indicated. Strike it and release the bend back to the original note.

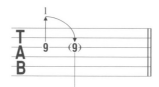

UNISON BEND: Strike the two notes simultaneously and bend the lower note up to the pitch of the higher.

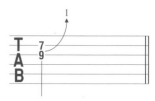

HOLD BEND: While sustaining bent note, strike note on different string.

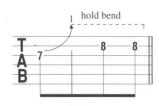

VIBRATO: The string is vibrated by rapidly bending and releasing the note with the fretting hand.

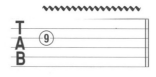

WIDE VIBRATO: The pitch is varied to a greater degree by vibrating with the fretting hand.

HAMMER-ON: Strike the first (lower) note with one finger, then sound the higher note (on the same string) with another finger by fretting it without picking.

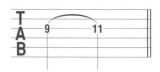

PULL-OFF: Place both fingers on the notes to be sounded. Strike the first note and without picking, pull the finger off to sound the second (lower) note.

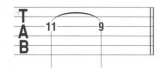

HAMMER FROM NOWHERE: Sound note(s) by hammering with fret hand finger only.

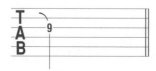

GRACE NOTE SLUR: Strike the note and immediately hammer-on (or pull-off) as indicated.

GRACE NOTE SLUR (CLUSTER): Strike the notes and immediately hammer-on (or pull-off) as indicated.

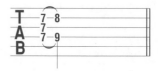

LEGATO SLIDE: Strike the first note and then slide the same fret-hand finger up or down to the second note. The second note is not struck.

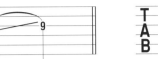

SHIFT SLIDE: Same as legato slide, except the second note is struck.

TRILL: Very rapidly alternate between the notes indicated by continuously hammering on and pulling off.

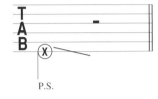

TAPPING: Hammer ("tap") the fret indicated with the pick-hand index or middle finger and pull off to the note fretted by the fret hand.

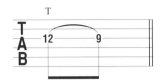

NATURAL HARMONIC: Strike the note while the fret-hand lightly touches the string directly over the fret indicated.

Harm.

PINCH HARMONIC: The note is fretted normally and a harmonic is produced by adding the edge of the thumb or the tip of the index finger of the pick hand to the normal pick attack.

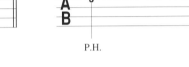

P.H.

HARP HARMONIC: The note is fretted normally and a harmonic is produced by gently resting the pick hand's index finger directly above the indicated fret (in parentheses) while the pick hand's thumb or pick assists by plucking the appropriate string.

H.H.

PICK SCRAPE: The edge of the pick is rubbed down (or up) the string, producing a scratchy sound.

P.S.

MUFFLED STRINGS: A percussive sound is produced by laying the fret hand across the string(s) without depressing, and striking them with the pick hand.

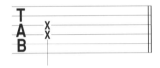

PALM MUTING: The note is partially muted by the pick hand lightly touching the string(s) just before the bridge.

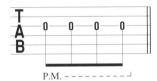

P.M. - - - - - - - - -

RAKE: Drag the pick across the strings indicated with a single motion.

rake - - ⌐

TREMOLO PICKING: The note is picked as rapidly and continuously as possible.

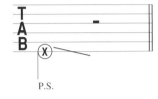

ARPEGGIATE: Play the notes of the chord indicated by quickly rolling them from bottom to top.

VIBRATO BAR DIVE AND RETURN: The pitch of the note or chord is dropped a specified number of steps (in rhythm), then returned to the original pitch.

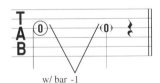

w/ bar -1

VIBRATO BAR SCOOP: Depress the bar just before striking the note, then quickly release the bar.

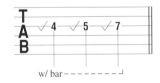

w/ bar - - - - - - - ⌐

VIBRATO BAR DIP: Strike the note and then immediately drop a specified number of steps, then release back to the original pitch.

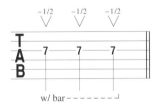

w/ bar - - - - - - - ⌐

Additional Musical Definitions

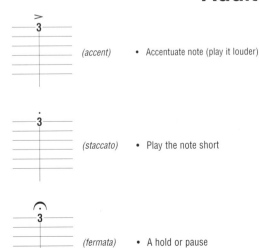

(accent) • Accentuate note (play it louder)

(staccato) • Play the note short

(fermata) • A hold or pause

 • Downstroke

V • Upstroke

 • Repeat measures between signs

---

NOTE: Tablature numbers in parentheses are used when:
- The note is sustained, but a new articulation begins (such as a hammer-on, pull-off, slide, or bend), or
- A bend is released.

Alice's Restaurant

Words and Music by Arlo Guthrie

Capo II

Key of D (Capo Key of C)

Intro

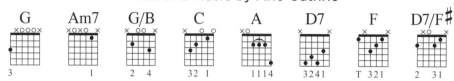

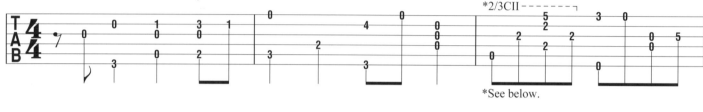

*See below.

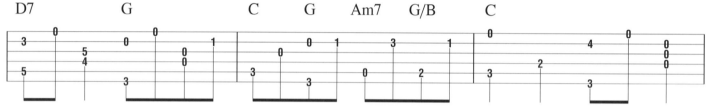

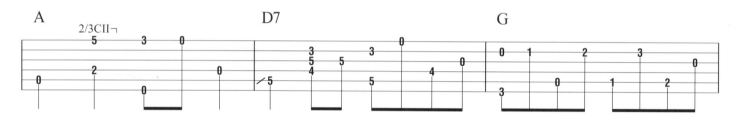

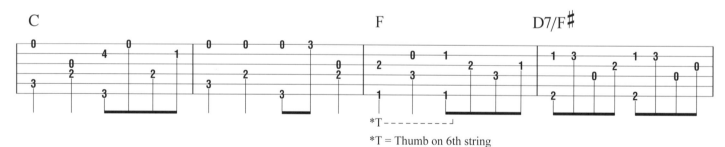

*T = Thumb on 6th string

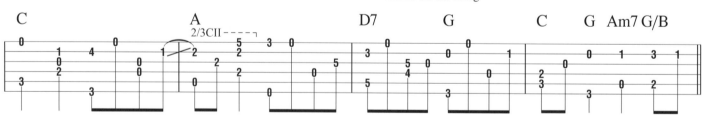

Verse

Spoken over Intro pattern, 1 time:

1. *This song is called Alice's Restaurant, and it's about Alice, and the restaurant, but Alice's Restaurant is not the name of the restaurant, that's just the name of the song, and that's why I called the song Alice's Restaurant.*

*"C" denotes barre. Fractional prefix indicates which strings are barred (e.g. 1/2 = first 3 strings).
  Roman numeral suffix indicates barred fret.

𝄋 Chorus

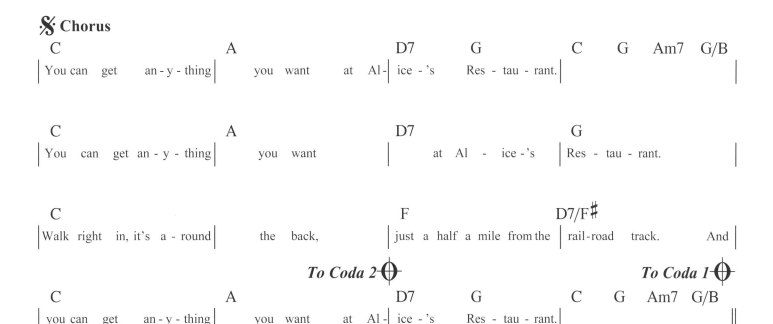

```
  C                        A                    D7      G          C    G   Am7  G/B
| You can  get  an-y-thing |      you   want    at Al- ice -'s  Res - tau - rant. |              |

  C                        A                    D7                 G
| You  can  get an-y-thing |      you   want    |     at Al - ice -'s | Res - tau - rant. |          |

  C                                             F              D7/F♯
| Walk  right  in,  it's a-round |   the   back,  | just a half a mile from the | rail-road   track.       And |
```

                        To Coda 2 ⊕   *To Coda 1* ⊕
```
  C                        A                    D7      G          C    G   Am7  G/B
| you can  get   an-y-thing |     you   want    at Al- ice -'s  Res - tau - rant. |              ‖
```

Verse

Spoken over Intro pattern, repeat as needed:

2. Now it all started two Thanksgivings ago, was on - two years ago on Thanksgiving, when my friend and I went up to visit Alice at the restaurant, but Alice doesn't live in the restaurant, she lives in the church nearby the restaurant, in the bell tower, with her husband Ray and Fasha the dog. And livin' in the bell tower like that, they got a lot of room downstairs where the pews used to be in. Havin' all that room, seein' as how they took out all the pews, they decided that they didn't have to take out their garbage for a long time.

We got up there, we found all the garbage in there, and we decided it'd be a friendly gesture for us to take the garbage down to the city dump. So we took the half a ton of garbage, put it in the back of a red VW microbus, took shovels and rakes and implements of destruction and headed on toward the city dump.

Well, we got there and there was a big sign and a chain across the dump saying, "Closed on Thanksgiving." And we had never heard of a dump closed on Thanksgiving before, and with tears in our eyes we drove off into the sunset looking for another place to put the garbage.

We didn't find one. Till we came to a side road, and off the side of the side road was another fifteen foot cliff and at the bottom of the cliff was another pile of garbage. And we decided that one big pile is better than two little piles, and rather than bring that one up we decided to throw ours down.

That's what we did, and drove back to the church, had a Thanksgiving dinner that couldn't be beat, went to sleep and didn't get up until the next morning, when we got a phone call from officer Obie. He said, "Kid, we found your name on an envelope at the bottom of a half a ton of garbage, and just wanted to know if you had any information about it." And I said, "Yes, sir, Officer Obie, I cannot tell a lie, I put that envelope under that garbage."

After speaking to Obie for about forty-five minutes on the telephone we finally arrived at the truth of the matter and said that we had to go down and pick up the garbage, and also had to go down and speak to him at the police officer's station. So we got in the red VW microbus with the shovels and rakes and implements of destruction and headed on toward the police officer's station.

Now friends, there was only one or two things that Obie coulda done at the police station, and the first was that he coulda give us a medal for being so brave and honest on the telephone, which wasn't very likely, and we didn't expect it, and the other thing was that he could have bawled us out and told us never to be seen driving garbage around the vicinity again, which is what we expected, but when we got to the police officer's station there was a third possibility that we hadn't even counted upon, and we was both immediately arrested. Handcuffed. And I said "Obie, I don't think I can pick up the garbage with these handcuffs on." He said, "Shut up, kid. Get in the back of the patrol car."

And that's what we did, sat in the back of the patrol car and drove to the quote "Scene of the Crime" unquote. I want tell you about the town of Stockbridge, Massachusetts, where this happened here, they got three stop signs, two police officers, and one police car, but when we got to the Scene of the Crime there was five police officers and three police cars, being the biggest crime of the last fifty years, and everybody wanted to get in the newspaper story about it. And they was using up all kinds of cop equipment that they had hanging around the police officer's station. They was taking plaster tire tracks, foot prints, dog smelling prints, and they took twenty-seven eight-by-ten colour glossy photographs with circles and arrows and a paragraph on the back of each one explaining what each one was to be used as evidence against us. Took pictures of the approach, the getaway, the northwest corner, the southwest corner and that's not to mention the aerial photography.

After the ordeal, we went back to the jail. Obie said he was going to put us in the cell. Said, "Kid, I'm going to put you in the cell, I want your wallet and your belt." And I said, "Obie, I can understand you wanting my wallet so I don't have any money to spend in the cell, but what do you want my belt for?" And he said, "Kid, we don't want any hangings." I said, "Obie, did you think I was going to hang myself for littering?" Obie said he was just making sure, and friends, Obie was, cause he took out the toilet seat so I couldn't hit myself over the head and drown, and he took out the toilet paper so I couldn't bend the bars, roll out the - roll the toilet paper out the window, slide down the roll and have an escape. Obie was making sure, and it was about four or five hours later that Alice (remember Alice? It's a song about Alice), Alice came by and with a few nasty words to Obie on the side, bailed us out of jail, and we went back to the church, had another Thanksgiving dinner that couldn't be beat, and didn't get up until the next morning, when we all had to go to court.

We walked in, sat down, Obie came in with the twenty-seven eight-by-ten colour glossy pictures with circles and arrows and a paragraph on the back of each one 'n' sat down. Man came in, said, "All rise." We all stood up, and Obie stood up with the twenty-seven eight-by-ten colour glossy pictures, and the judge walked in, sat down with a seeing eye dog, and he sat down; we sat down. Obie looked at the seeing eye dog, and then at the twenty-seven eight-by-ten colour glossy pictures with circles and arrows and a paragraph on the back of each one, and looked at the seeing eye dog. And then at twenty-seven eight-by-ten colour glossy pictures with circles and arrows and a paragraph on the back of each one and began to cry, 'cause Obie came to the realization that it was a typical case of American blind justice, and there wasn't nothing he could do about it, and the judge wasn't going to look at the twenty-seven eight-by-ten colour glossy pictures with the circles and arrows and a paragraph on the back of each one explaining what each one was to be used as evidence against us. And we was fined fifty dollars and had to pick up the garbage in the snow, but that's not what I came to tell you about.

Came to talk about the draft.

They got a building down New York City, it's called Whitehall Street, where you walk in, you get injected, inspected, detected, infected, neglected and selected. I went down to get my physical examination one day, and I walked in, I sat down, got good and drunk the night before, so I looked and felt my best when I went in that morning. 'Cause I wanted to look like the all-American kid from New York City, man I wanted, I wanted to feel like the all-, I wanted to be the all-American kid from New York, and I walked in, sat down, I was hung down, brung down, hung up, and all kinds o' mean nasty ugly things. And I walked in and sat down and they gave me a piece of paper, said, "Kid, see the psychiatrist, room six-O-four." And I went up there, I said, "Shrink, I want to kill. I mean, I wanna, I wanna kill. Kill. I wanna, I wanna see, I wanna see blood and gore and guts and veins in my teeth. Eat dead burnt bodies. I mean kill, KILL, KILL, KILL." And I started jumpin' up and down yelling, "KILL, KILL," and he started jumpin' up and down with me and we was both jumpin' up and down yelling, "KILL, KILL." And the Sergeant came over, pinned a medal on me, sent me down the hall, said, "You're our boy."

Didn't feel too good about it.

Proceeded on down the hall gettin' more injections, inspections, detections, neglections and all kinds of stuff that they was doin' to me at the thing there, and I was there for two hours, three hours, four hours, I was there for a long time going through all kinds of mean nasty ugly things and I was just having a tough time there, and they was inspecting, injecting every single part of me, and they was leaving no part untouched. Proceeded through, and when I finally came to see the very last man, I walked in, walked in, sat down after a whole big thing there, and I walked up and said, "What do you want?" He said, "Kid, we only got one question: have you ever been arrested?"

And I proceeded to tell him the story of the Alice's Restaurant Massacre, with full orchestration and five part harmony and stuff like that and all the phenome... - and he stopped me right there and said, "Kid, did you ever go to court?"

And I proceeded to tell him the story of the twenty-seven eight-by-ten colour glossy pictures with the circles and arrows and the paragraph on the back of each one, and he stopped me right there and said, "Kid, I want you to go over and sit down on that bench that says Group W .... NOW kid!!"

And I, I walked over to the, to the bench there, and there is, Group W's where they put you if you may not be moral enough to join the army after committing your special crime, and there was all kinds of mean, nasty, ugly looking people on the bench there: mother rapers, father stabbers, father rapers! Father rapers sitting right there on the bench next to me! And they was mean and nasty and ugly and horrible crime-type guys just sitting there on the bench. And the meanest, ugliest, nastiest one, the meanest father raper of them all, was coming over to me and he was mean 'n' ugly 'n' nasty 'n' horrible and all kind of things and he sat down next to me and said, "Kid, whad'ya get?" I said, "I didn't get nothing, I had to pay fifty dollars and pick up the garbage." He said, "What were you arrested for, kid?" And I said, "Littering." And they all moved away from me on the bench there, and the hairy eyeball and all kinds of mean nasty things, till I said, "And creating a nuisance." And they all came back, shook my hand, and we had a great time on the bench, talkin' about crime, mother stabbing, father raping, all kinds of groovy things that we was talking about on the bench. And everything was fine, we was smoking cigarettes and all kinds of things, until the Sergeant came over, had some paper in his hand, held it up and said:

"Kids, this-piece-of-paper's-got-forty-seven-words-thirty-seven-sentences-fifty-eight-words-we-wanna-know-details-of-the-crime-time-of-the-crime-and-any-other-kind-of-thing-you-gotta-say-pertaining-to-and-about-the-crime-I-want-to-know-arresting-officer's-name-and-any-other-kind-of-thing-you-gotta-say," and talked for forty-five minutes and nobody understood a word that he said, but we had fun filling out the forms and playing with the pencils on the bench there, and I filled out the massacre with the four part harmony, and wrote it down there, just like it was, and ev'rything was fine and I put down the pencil, and I turned over the piece of paper, and, and there, there on the other side, in the middle of the other side, away from ev'rything else on the other side, in parentheses, capital letters, quoted, read the following words: "Kid, have you rehabilitated yourself?"*

I went over to the Sergeant, said, "Sergeant, you got a lotta damn gall to ask me if I've rehabilitated myself, I mean, I mean, I mean that just, I'm sittin' here on the bench, I mean I'm sittin here on the Group W bench 'cause you want to know if I'm moral enough join the army, burn women, kids, houses and villages after bein' a litterbug." He looked at me and said, "Kid, we don't like your kind, and we're gonna send your fingerprints off to Washington." And friends, somewhere in Washington enshrined in some little folder, is a study in black and white of my fingerprints. And the only reason I'm singing you this song now is cause you may know somebody in a similar situation, or you may be in a similar situation, and if you're in a situation like that there's only one thing you can do and that's walk into the shrink wherever you are, just walk in, say, "Shrink, (sung:) you can get anything you want, at Alice's restaurant." And walk out. You know, if one person, just one person does it they may think he's really sick and they won't take him. And if two people, two people do it, in harmony, they may think they're both faggots and they won't take either of them. And three people do it, three, can you imagine, three people walkin' in singin' a bar of Alice's Restaurant and walkin' out? They may think it's an organization. And can you, can you imagine fifty people a day, I said fifty people a day walkin' in singin' a bar of Alice's Restaurant and walking out? And friends, they may thinks it's a movement.

And that's what it is, the Alice's Restaurant Anti-Massacre Movement, and all you got to do to join is to sing it the next time it comes around on the guitar, with feeling. So we'll wait till it comes around on the guitar, here, and sing it when it does. Here it comes.

D.S. al Coda 1

Coda 1

Verse

Spoken over Intro pattern, repeat as needed:

3. *That was horrible. If you want to end war and stuff you got to sing loud. I've been singing this song now for twenty five minutes. I could sing it for another twenty five minutes. I'm not proud... or tired. So we'll wait till it comes around again, and this time with four part harmony and feeling. We're just waitin' for it to come around is what we're doing. All right now.*

D.S. al Coda 2

Coda 2

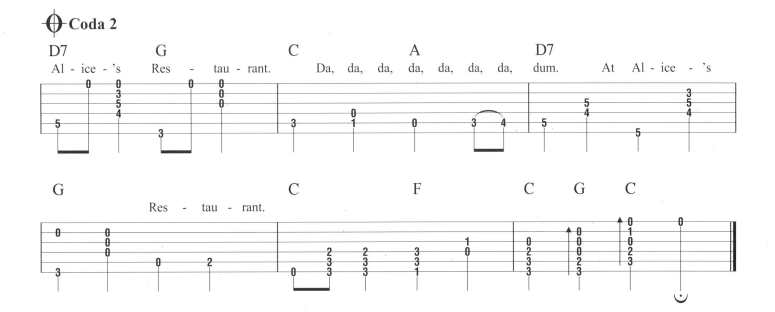

Annie's Song

Words and Music by John Denver

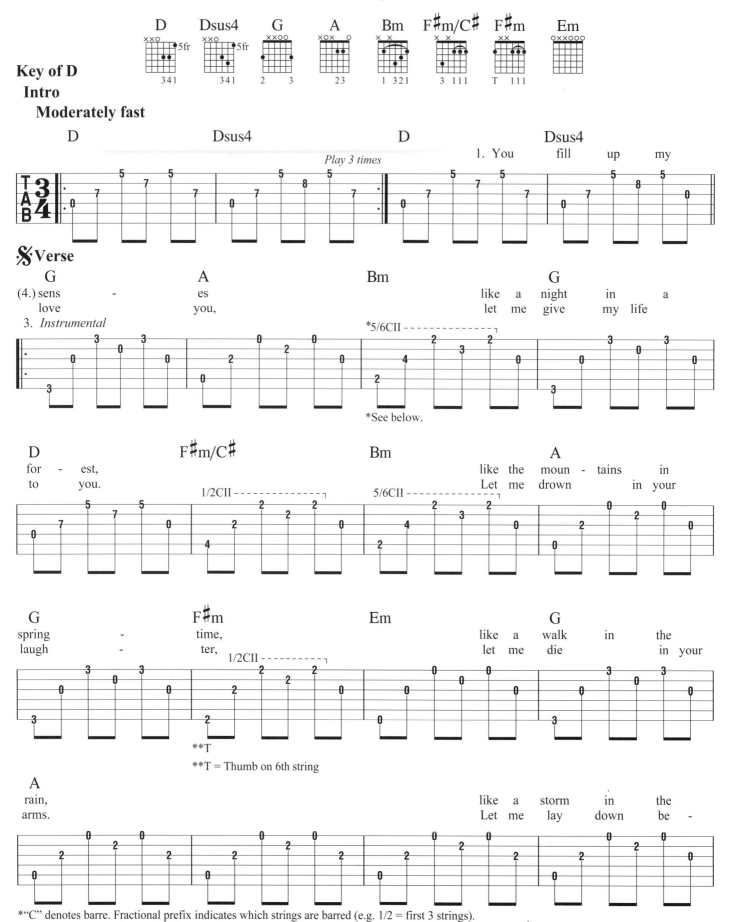

Key of D
Intro
   Moderately fast

4th time, To Coda ⊕

w/ Verse pattern

G	A	Bm	G
des - ert,	you,	like a sleep - y blue	let me al - ways be
side		*Instrumental ends* Let me give my life	

D	F#m/C#	Bm	A
o - cean.		You	fill up my
with you. ⎞		Come, let me	
to you. ⎠			

G	F#m	Em	
sens - es,		come	
love you,		come	

A	D	Dsus4	
fill me a - gain.			
love me a - gain.			

1., 2.

D	Dsus4
	2. Come let me
	3. *Instrumental*

3.   *D.S. al Coda*

D	Dsus4
	4. You fill up my

⊕ **Coda**

w/ picking pattern

Bm	D	F#m/C#
like the sleep - y blue	o - cean.	

Bm	A	G	F#m
You fill up my	sens - es,		

Em	A	D	Dsus4
come fill me a - gain.			

Outro

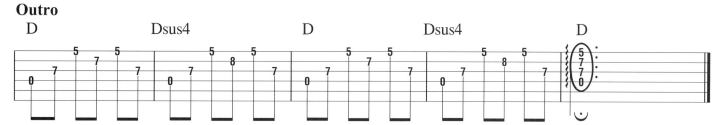

Babe, I'm Gonna Leave You

Words and Music by Anne Bredon, Jimmy Page and Robert Plant

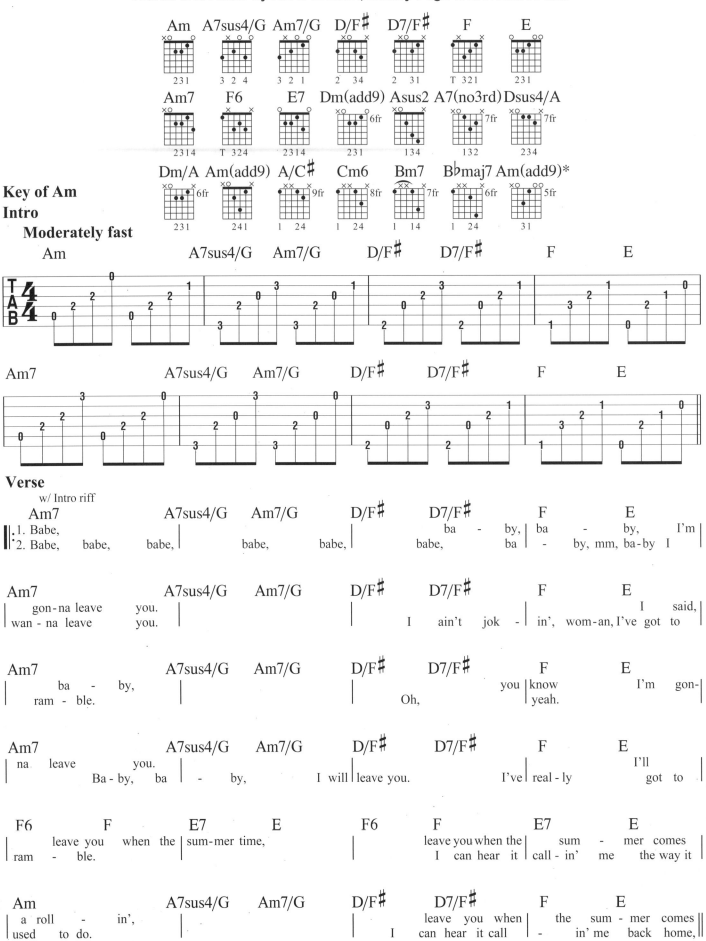

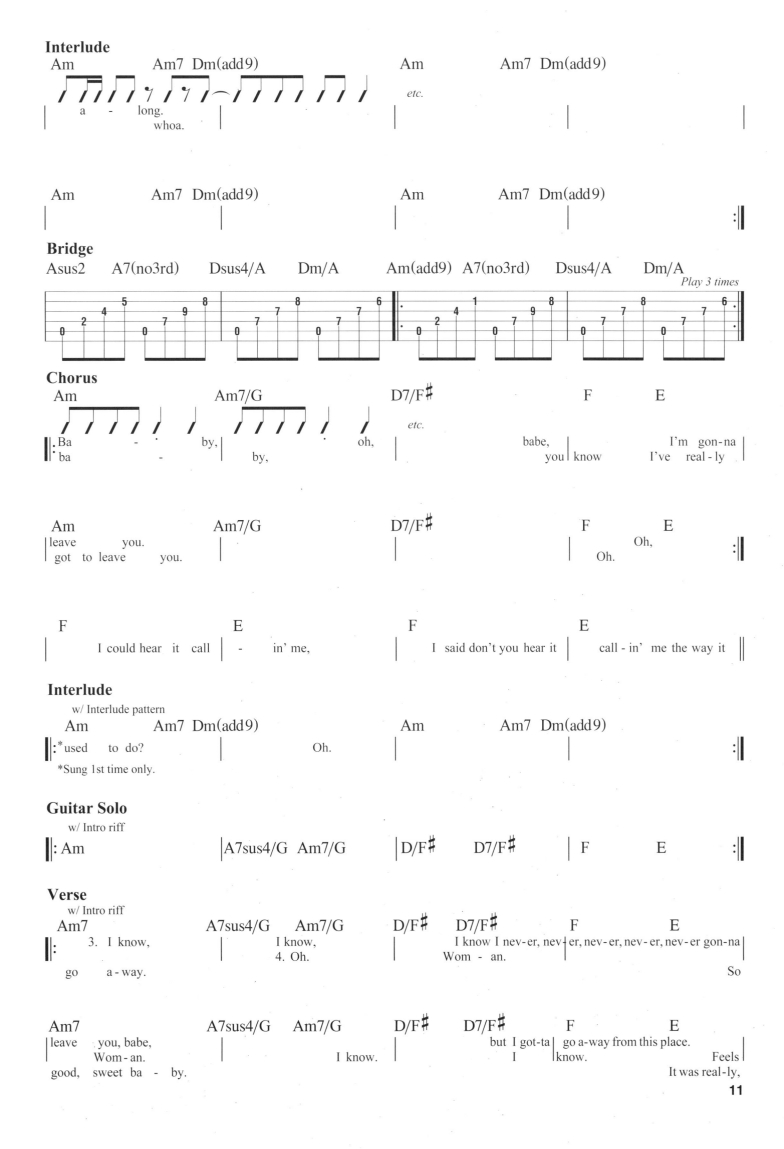

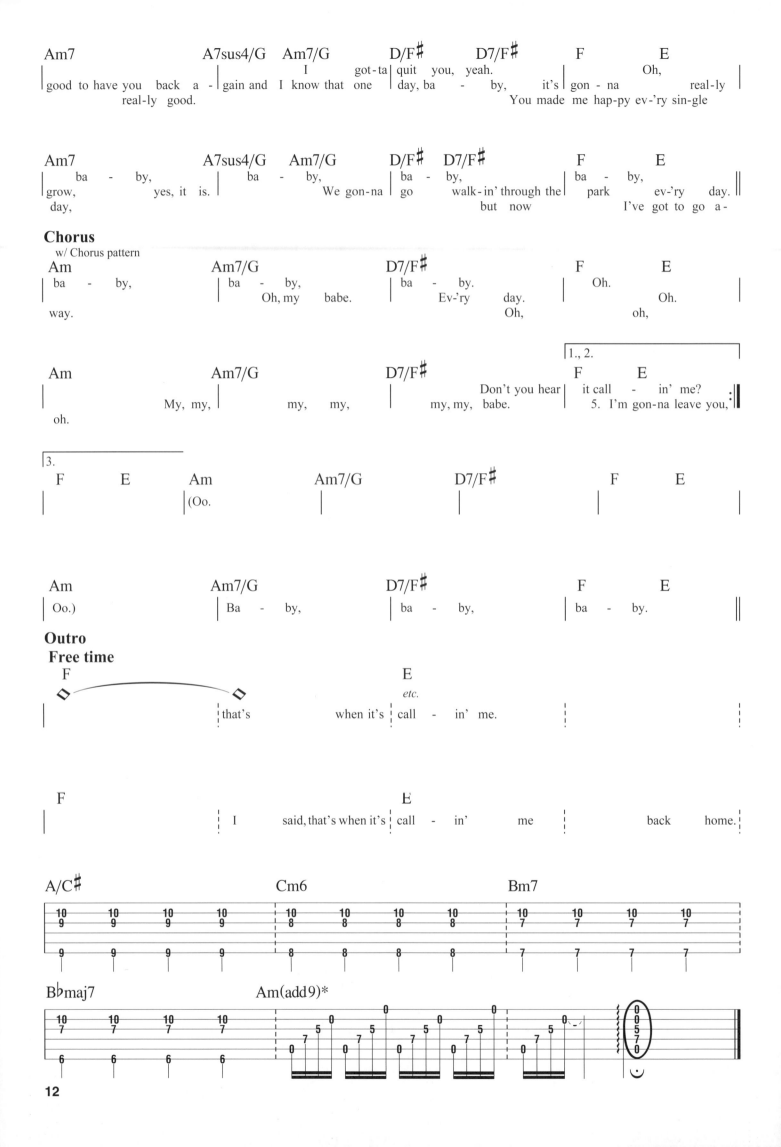

Blackbird

Words and Music by John Lennon and Paul McCartney

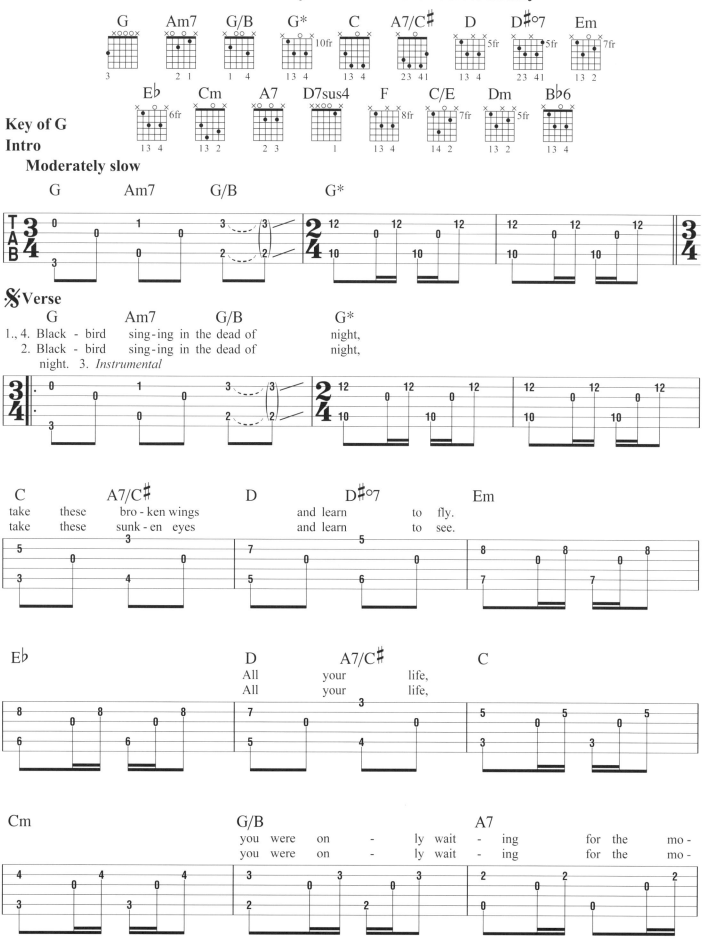

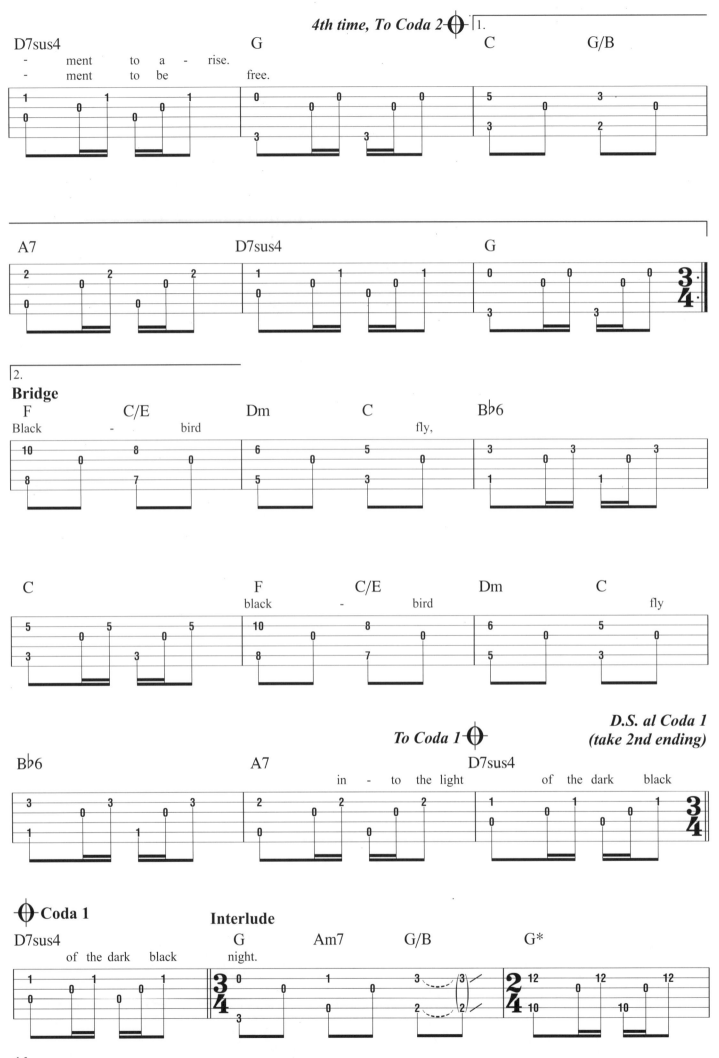

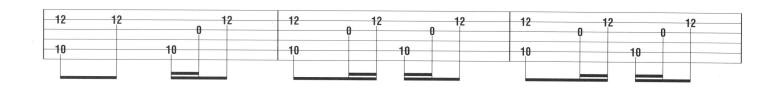

grad. slower

A tempo

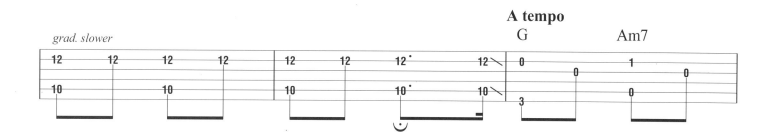

G   Am7

D.S. al Coda 2

G/B   C   G/B   A7   D7sus4

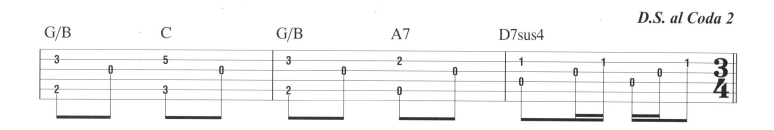

⊕ Coda 2

C   G/B   A7   D7sus4

You were on - ly   wait-ing   for this mo - ment to a - rise.

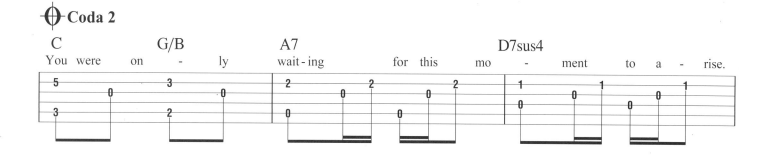

G   C   G/B   A7

You were on - ly wait-ing   for this mo -

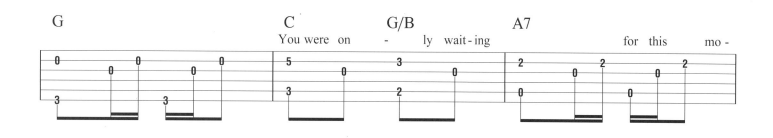

D7sus4   G

- ment   to a - rise.

grad. slower

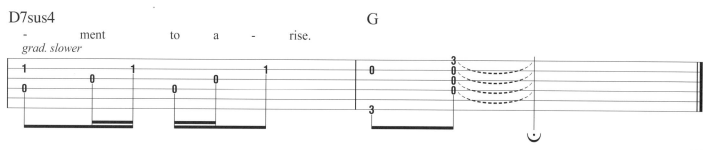

The Boxer

Words and Music by Paul Simon

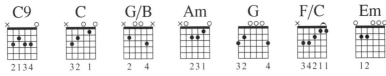

C9   C   G/B   Am   G   F/C   Em

2134   32 1   2 4   231   32 4   34211   12

*Tune down 1/2 step:
(low to high) E♭-A♭-D♭-G♭-B♭-E♭

Key of C
Intro

Moderately slow, in 2

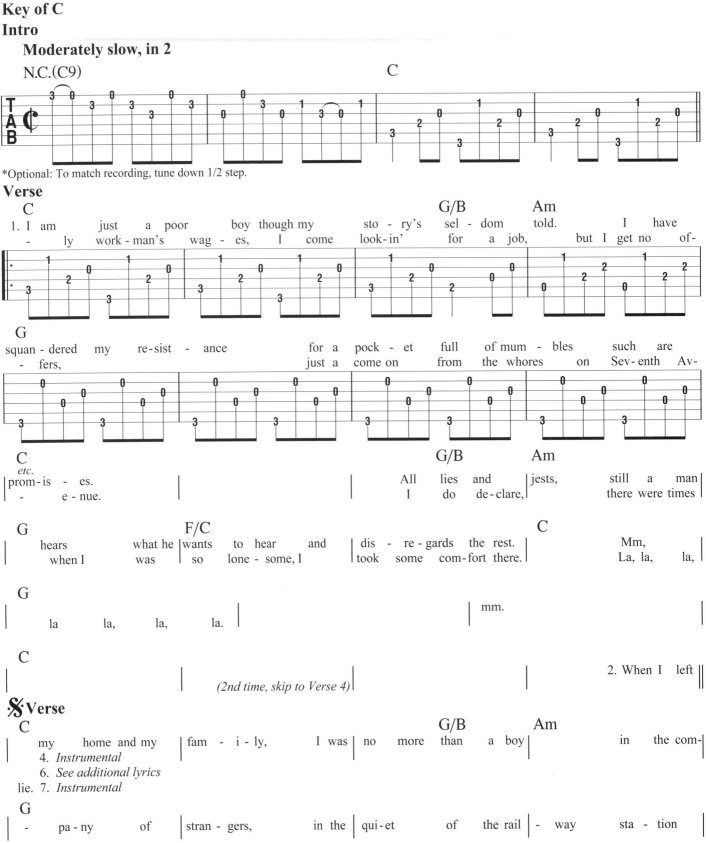

*Optional: To match recording, tune down 1/2 step.

Verse

C
1. I am   just   a poor   boy though my   sto - ry's   sel - dom   told.   I have
   - ly   work - man's   wag - es,   I   come   look - in'   for a   job,   but I get no of-

G
squan - dered my re-sist - ance   for a   pock - et   full   of mum - bles   such are
   - fers,   just a   come on   from the   whores   on   Sev - enth Av-

C
etc.
prom-is - es.   All   lies and   jests,   still a man
   - e - nue.   I   do de-clare,   there were times

G   F/C
hears   what he   wants to hear   and   dis - re - gards the rest.   Mm,
when I   was   so   lone - some, I   took   some com-fort there.   La, la,   la,

G
la   la,   la,   la.   mm.

C
                        (2nd time, skip to Verse 4)   2. When I   left

𝄋 Verse

C   G/B   Am
   my   home and my   fam - i - ly,   I was   no   more than a boy   in the com-
   4. *Instrumental*
   6. *See additional lyrics*
lie. 7. *Instrumental*

G
   - pa - ny   of   stran - gers,   in the   qui - et   of the rail   - way   sta - tion

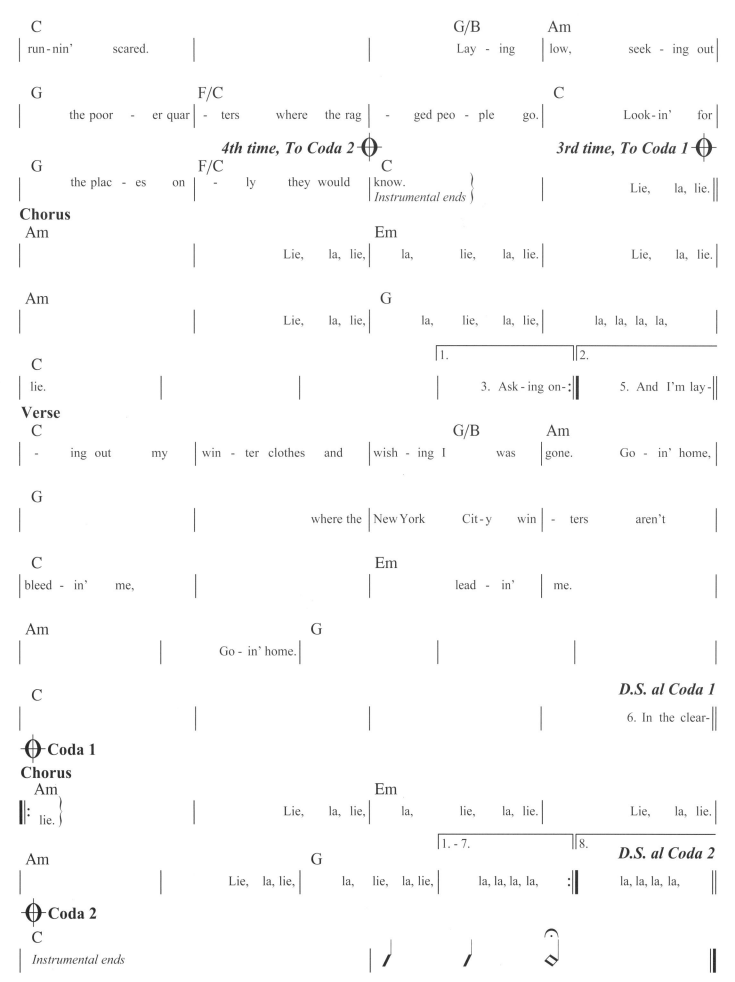

Additional Lyrics

6. In the clearing stands a boxer, and a fighter by his trade,
And he carries the reminders of every glove that laid him down
Or cut him 'til he cried out in his anger and his shame,
"I am leaving, I am leaving," but the fighter still remains, mm.

Can't Find My Way Home

Words and Music by Steve Winwood

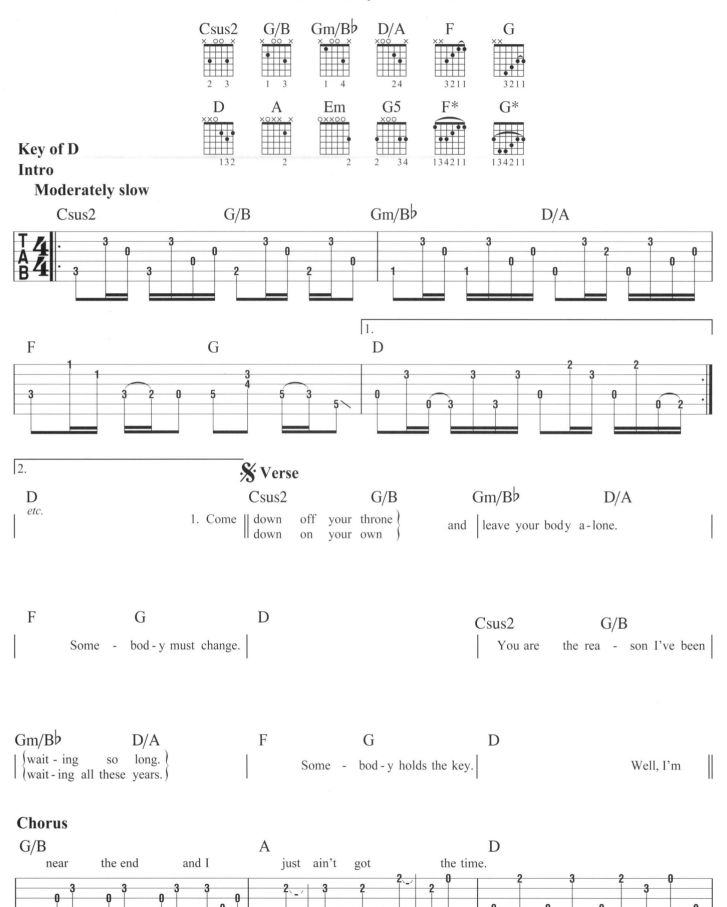

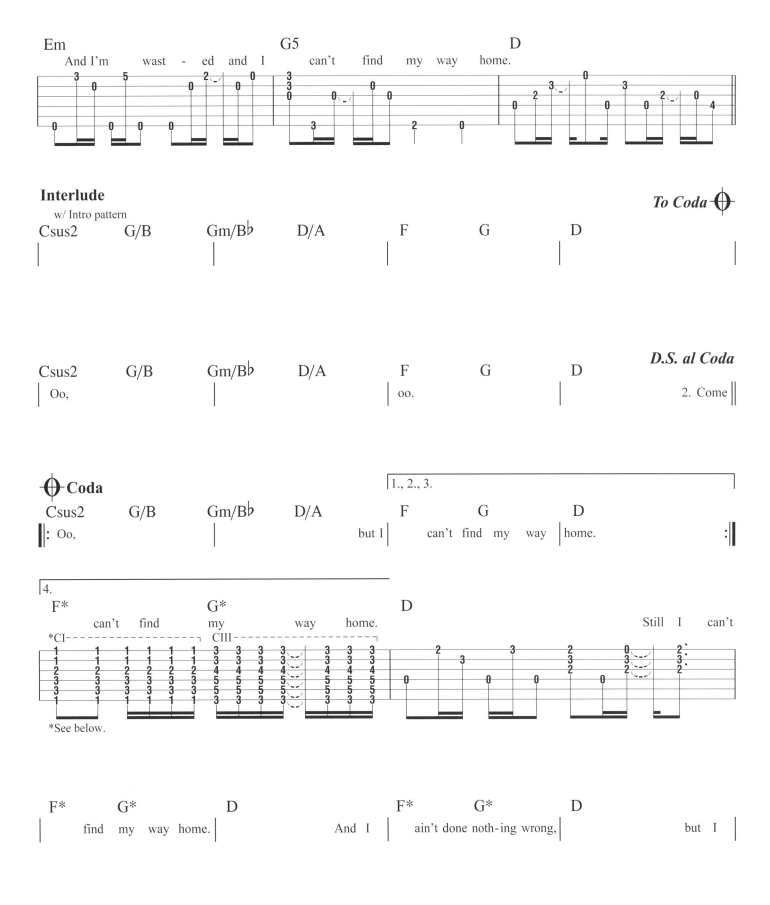

To Coda ⊕

Interlude
w/ Intro pattern

D.S. al Coda

⊕ **Coda**

"C" denotes barre. Fractional prefix indicates which strings are barred (e.g. 1/2 = first 3 strings).
Roman numeral suffix indicates barred fret.

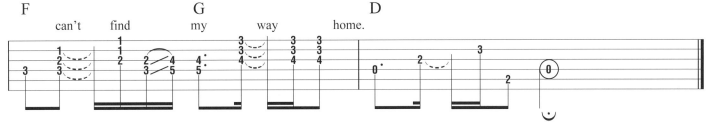

Cavatina

from the Universal Pictures and EMI Films Presentation THE DEER HUNTER
By Stanley Myers

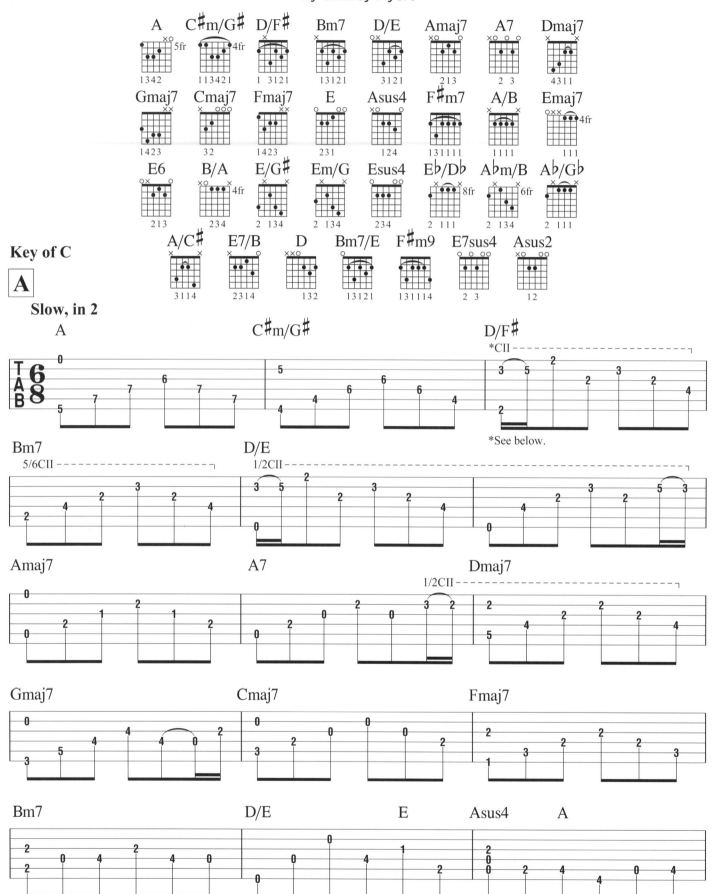

Key of C

[A]

Slow, in 2

*"C" denotes barre. Fractional prefix indicates which strings are barred (e.g. 1/2 = first 3 strings).
Roman numeral suffix indicates barred fret.

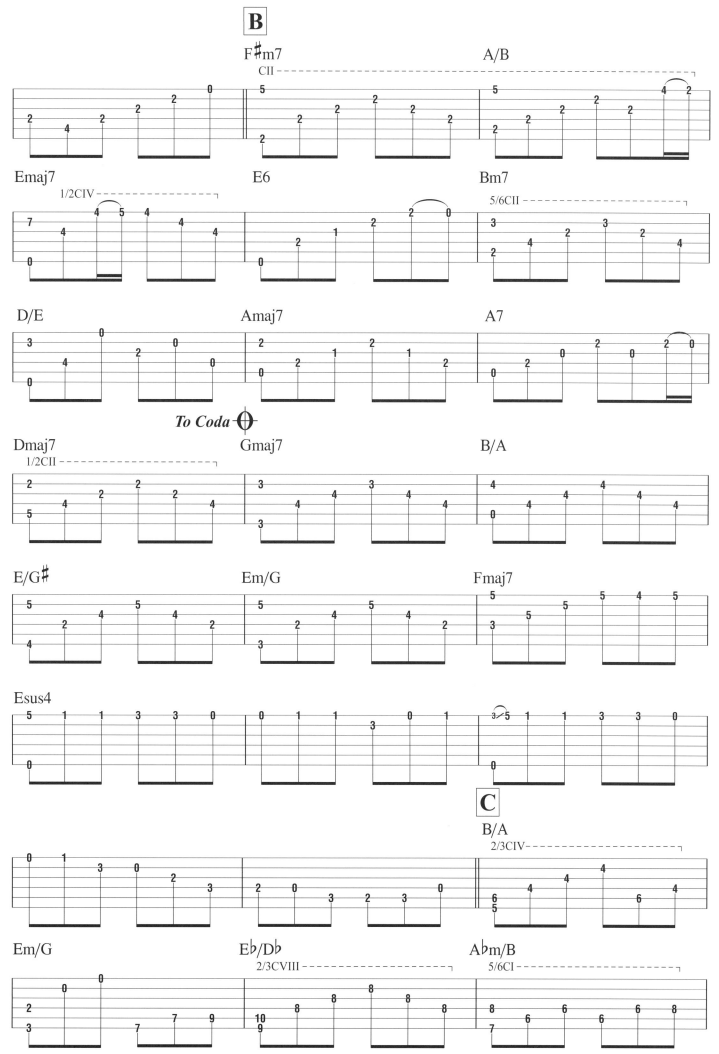

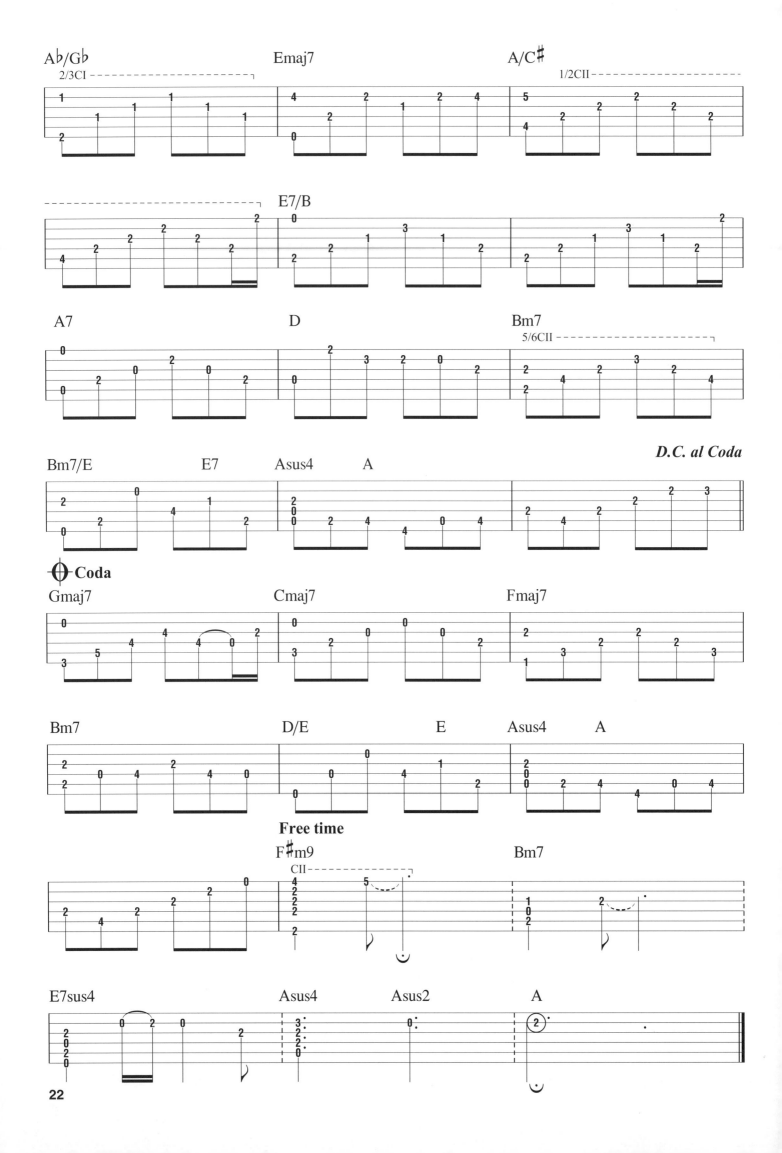

Desperate Man Blues

Written by John Fahey

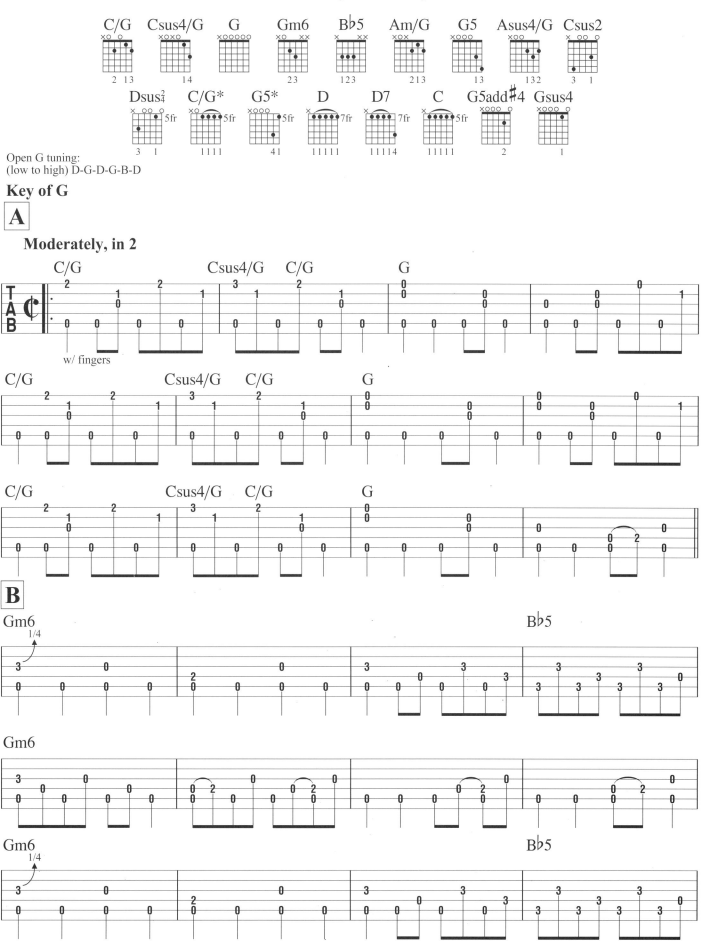

Open G tuning:
(low to high) D-G-D-G-B-D

Key of G

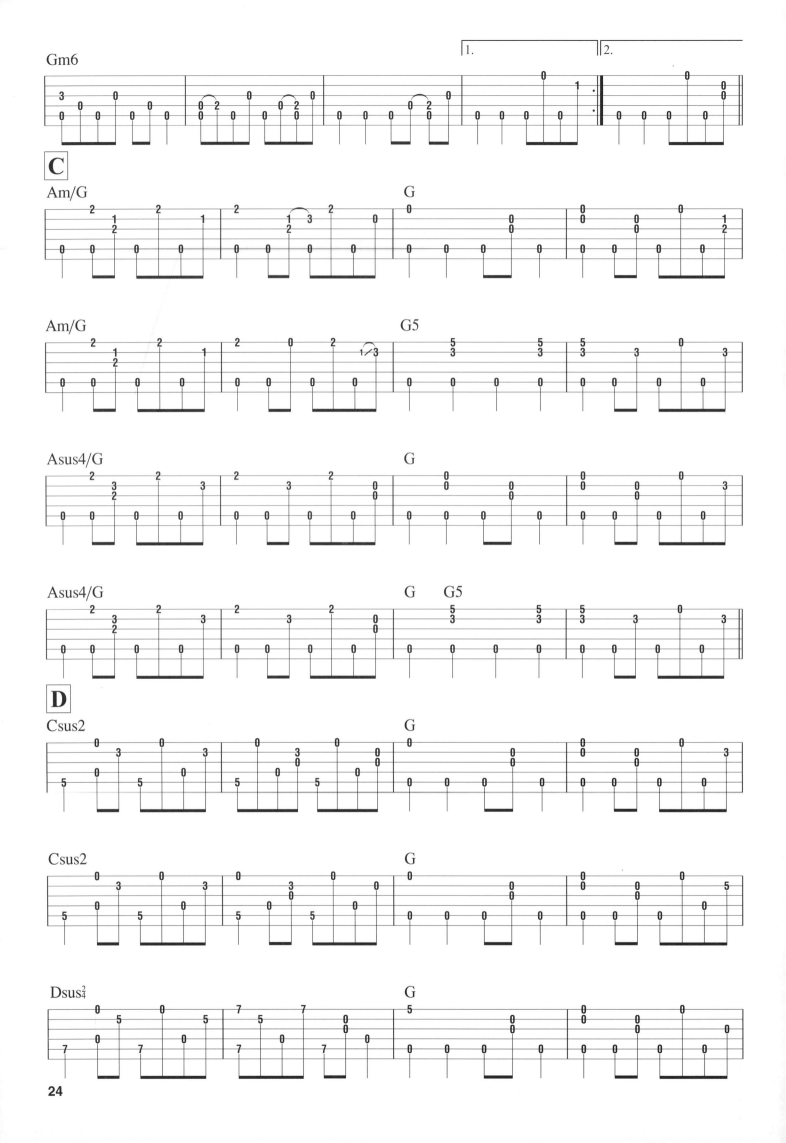

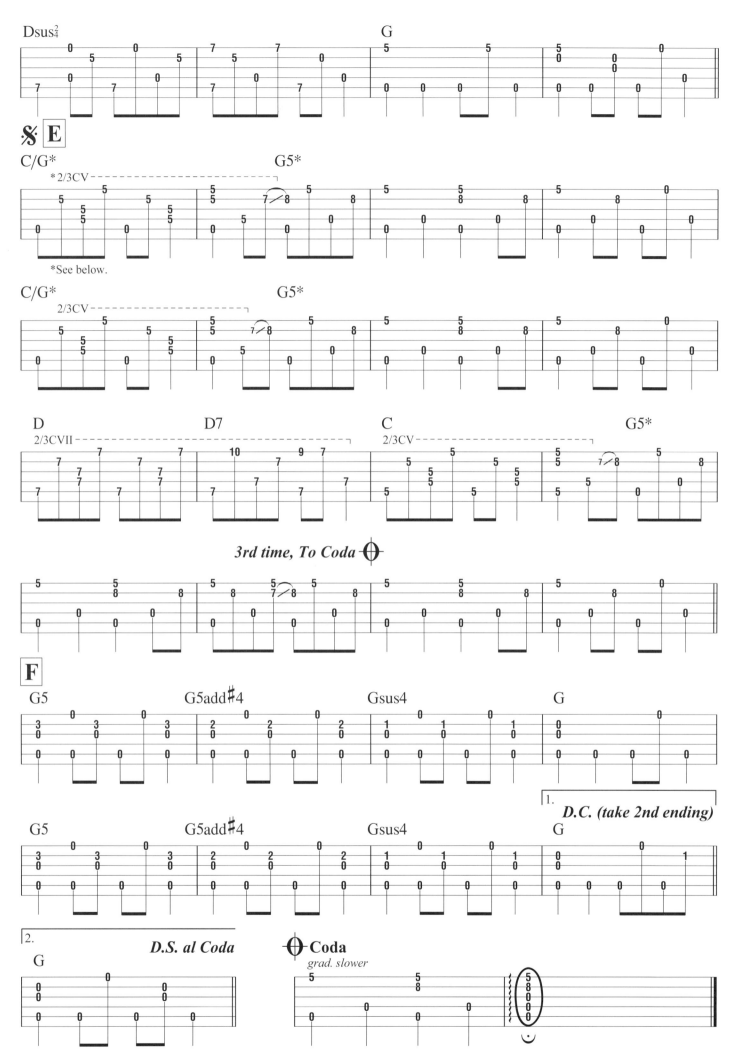

*"C" denotes barre. Fractional prefix indicates which strings are barred (e.g. 1/2 = first 3 strings).
Roman numeral suffix indicates barred fret.

Classical Gas

By Mason Williams

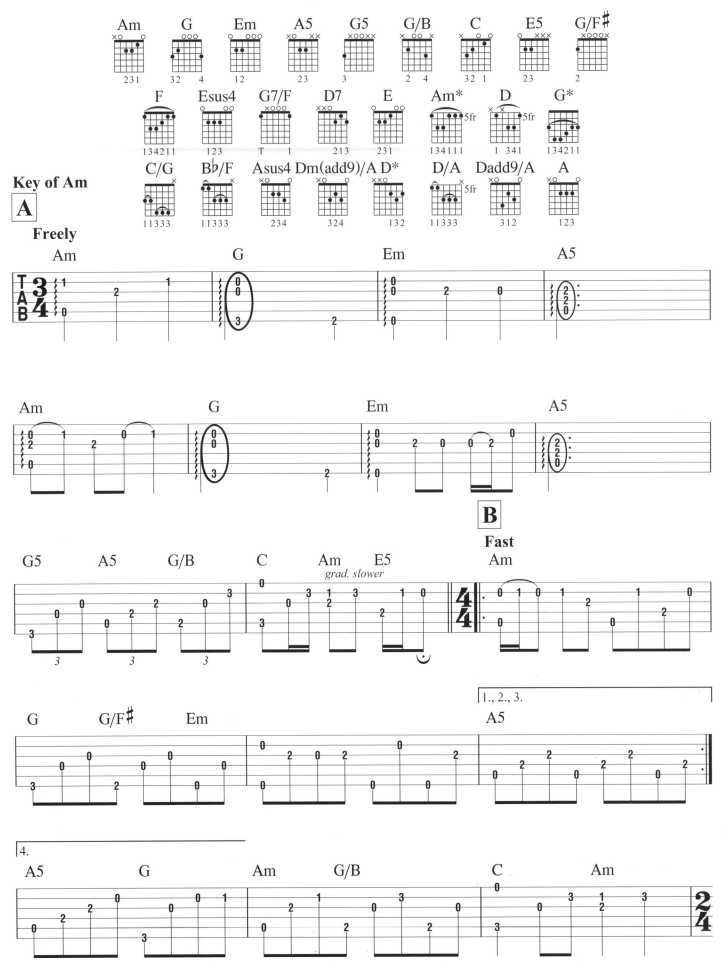

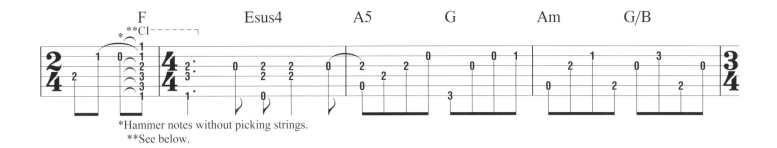

*Hammer notes without picking strings.
**See below.

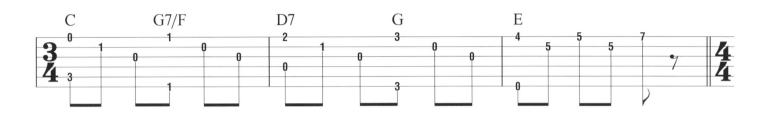

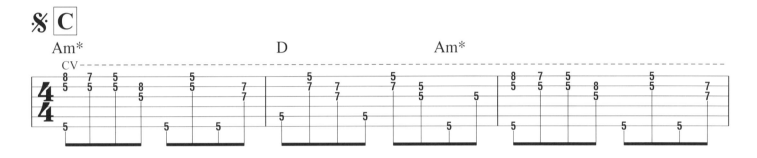

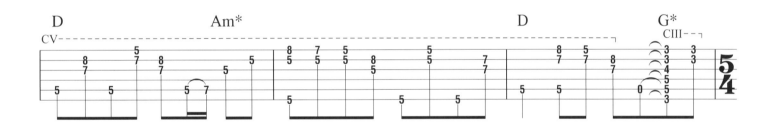

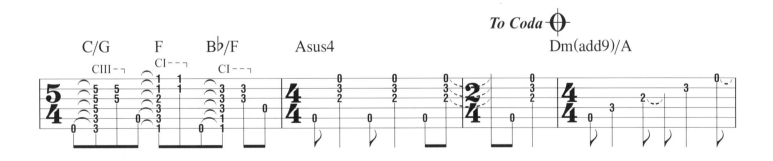

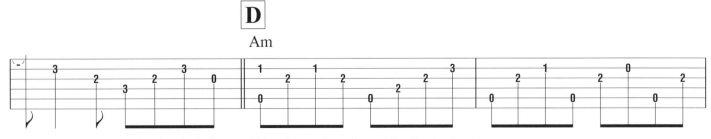

**"C" denotes barre. Fractional prefix indicates which strings are barred (e.g. 1/2 = first 3 strings).
Roman numeral suffix indicates barred fret.

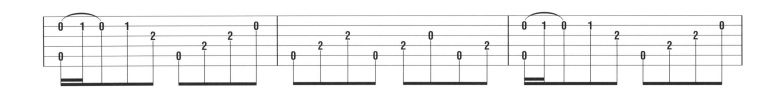

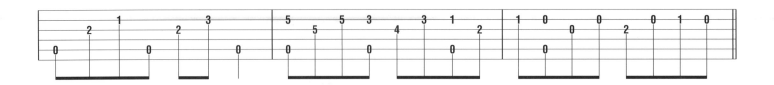

E

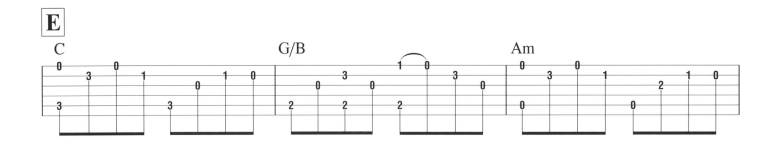

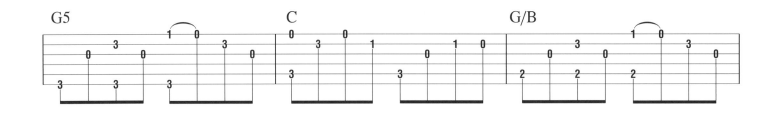

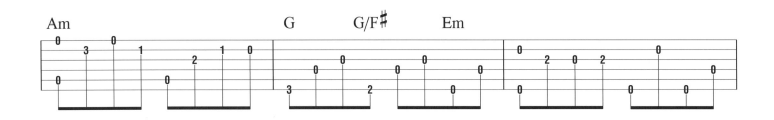

D.S. al Coda

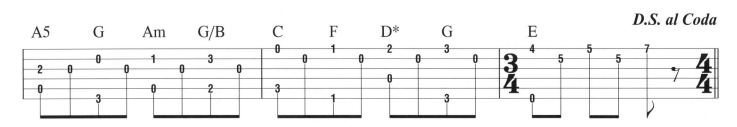

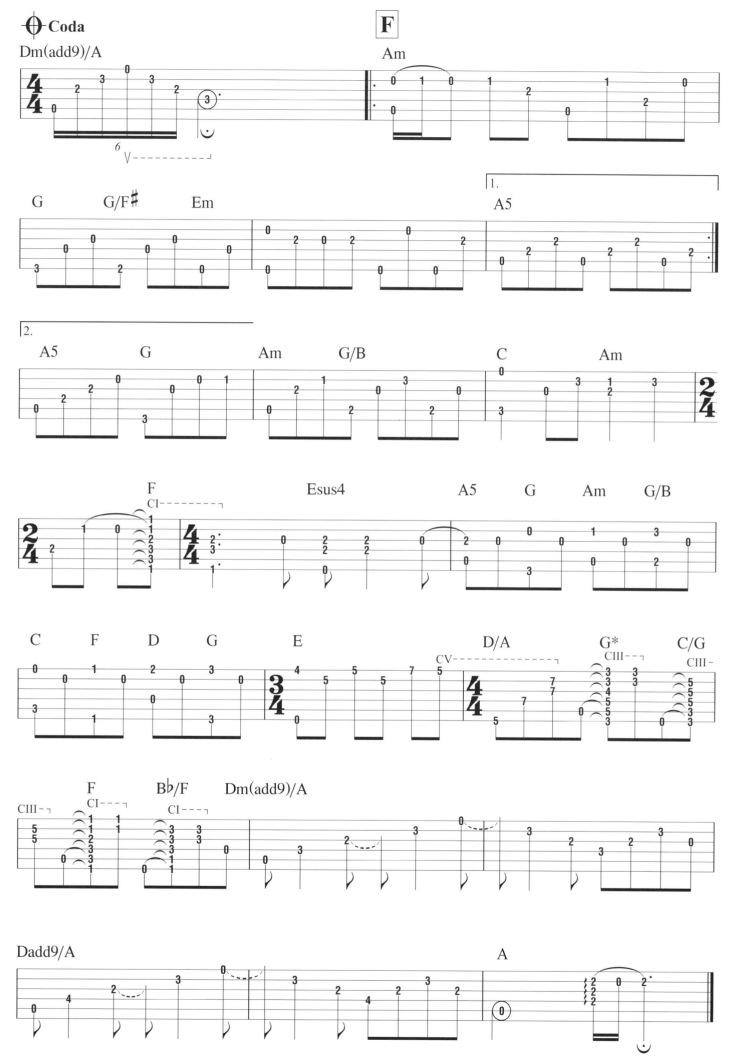

Danny's Song

Words and Music by Kenny Loggins

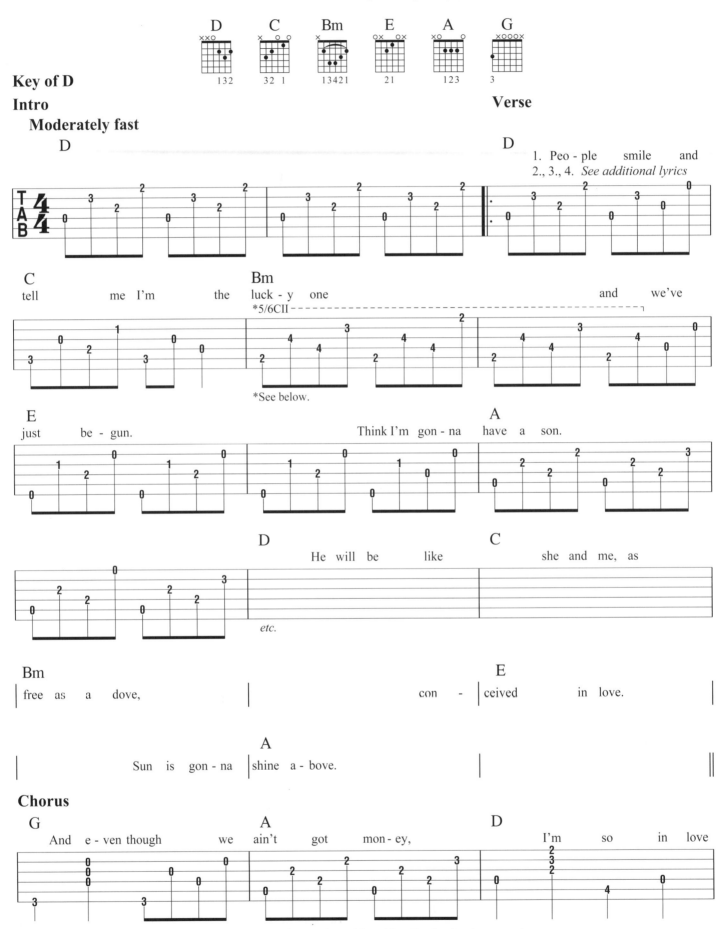

Key of D
Intro
Moderately fast

Verse

1. Peo - ple smile and
2., 3., 4. *See additional lyrics*

tell me I'm the luck - y one and we've

*5/6CII

*See below.

just be - gun. Think I'm gon - na have a son.

He will be like she and me, as

etc.

free as a dove, con - ceived in love.

Sun is gon - na shine a - bove.

Chorus

And e - ven though we ain't got mon - ey, I'm so in love

*"C" denotes barre. Fractional prefix indicates which strings are barred (e.g. 1/2 = first 3 strings).
Roman numeral suffix indicates barred fret.

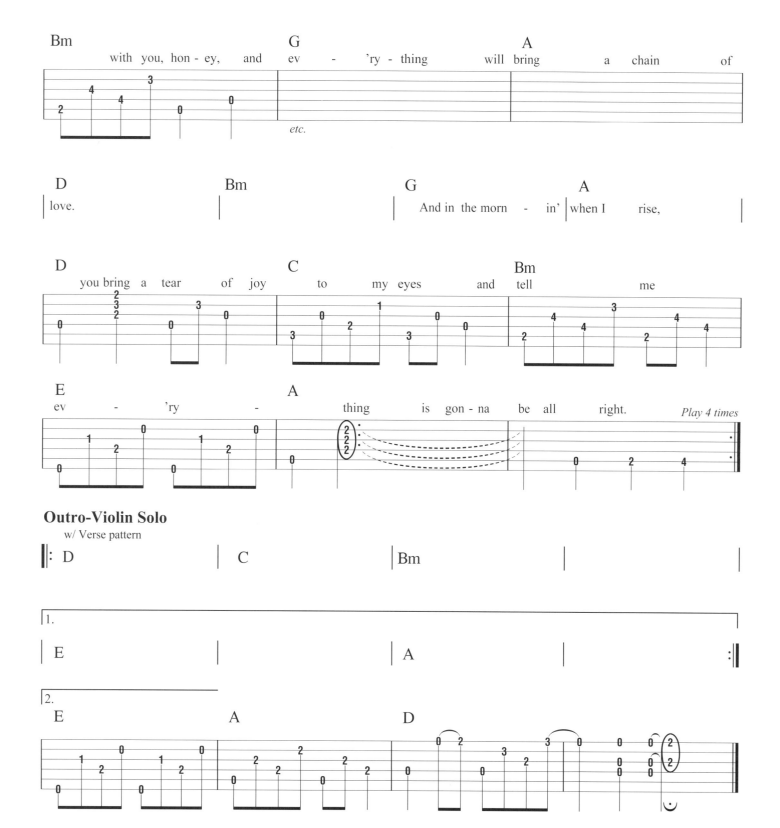

Additional Lyrics

2. Seems as though a month ago I was Beta Chi.
   Never got high; oh, I was a sorry guy.
   But now a smile, a face, a girl that shares my name, yeah.
   Now I'm through with the game; this boy'll never be the same.

3. Pisces, Virgo rising is a very good sign.
   Strong and kind, and the little boy is mine.
   Now I see a family where there once was none.
   Now we've just begun; yeah, we're gonna fly to the sun.

4. Love the girl who holds the world in a paper cup.
   Drink it up; love her and she'll bring you luck.
   And if you find she helps your mind, buddy, take her home.
   Don't you live alone; try to earn what lovers own.

Dear Prudence

Words and Music by John Lennon and Paul McCartney

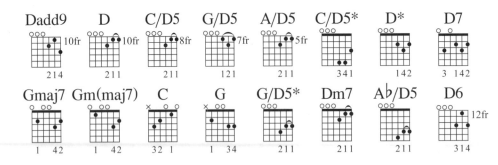

Drop D tuning:
(low to high) D-A-D-G-B-E

Key of D

Intro

Moderately slow

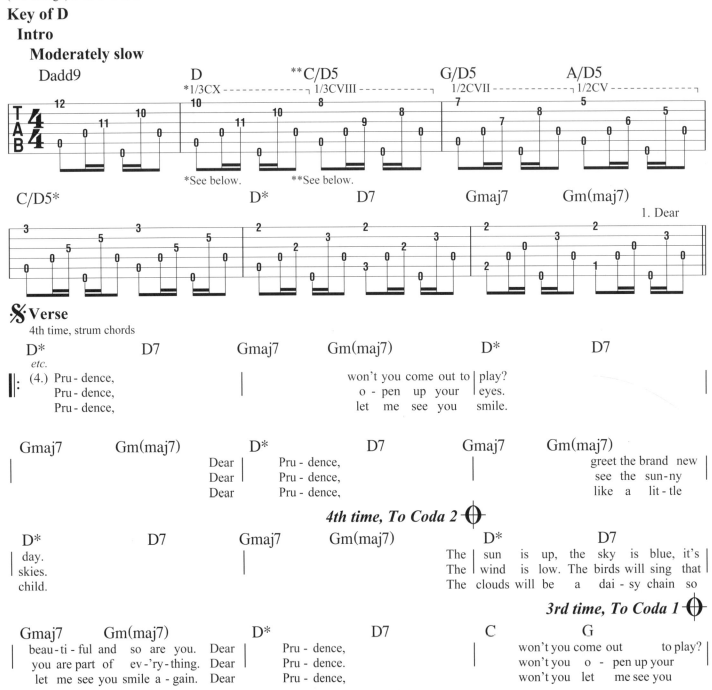

*"C" denotes barre. Fractional prefix indicates which strings are barred (e.g. 1/2 = first 3 strings).
Roman numeral suffix indicates barred fret.

In this arrangement, chord symbols ending in /D5 denote **polychords: two distinct chords played together, one above the other.

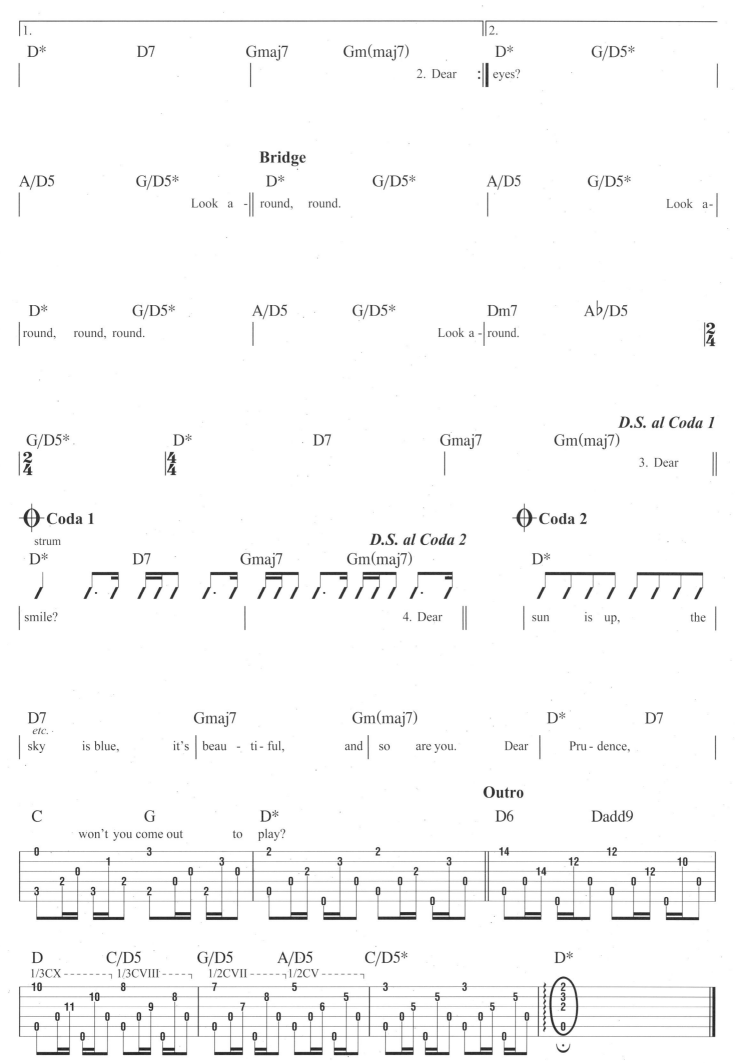

Deep River Blues

Traditional
Arranged and Adapted by Doc Watson

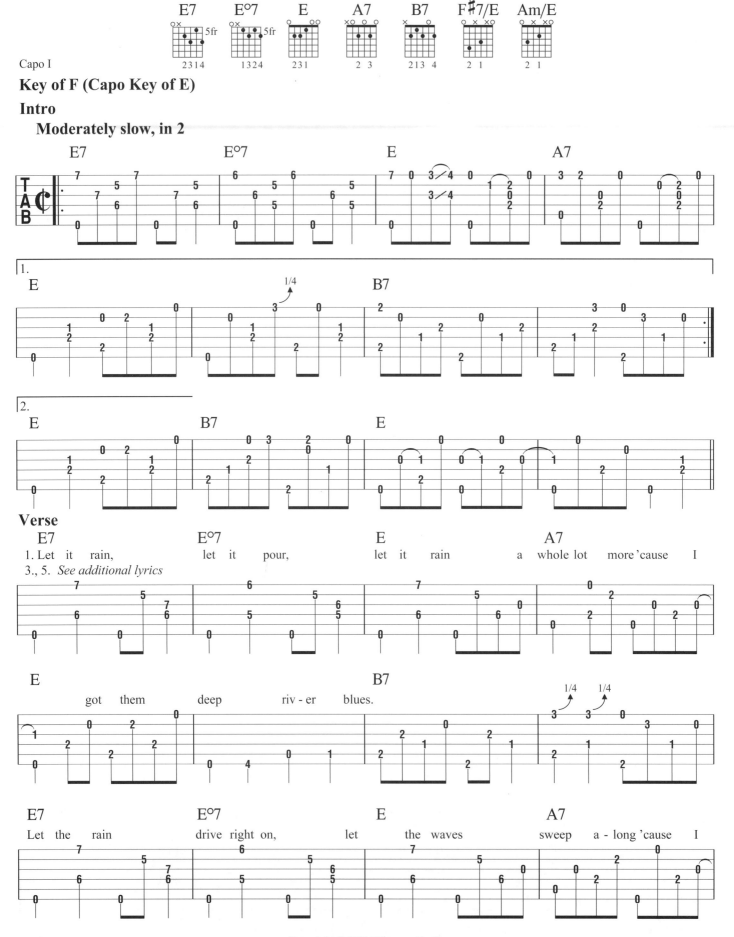

Capo I

Key of F (Capo Key of E)

Intro

Moderately slow, in 2

Verse

1. Let it rain, let it pour, let it rain a whole lot more 'cause I
3., 5. *See additional lyrics*

got them deep riv - er blues.

Let the rain drive right on, let the waves sweep a - long 'cause I

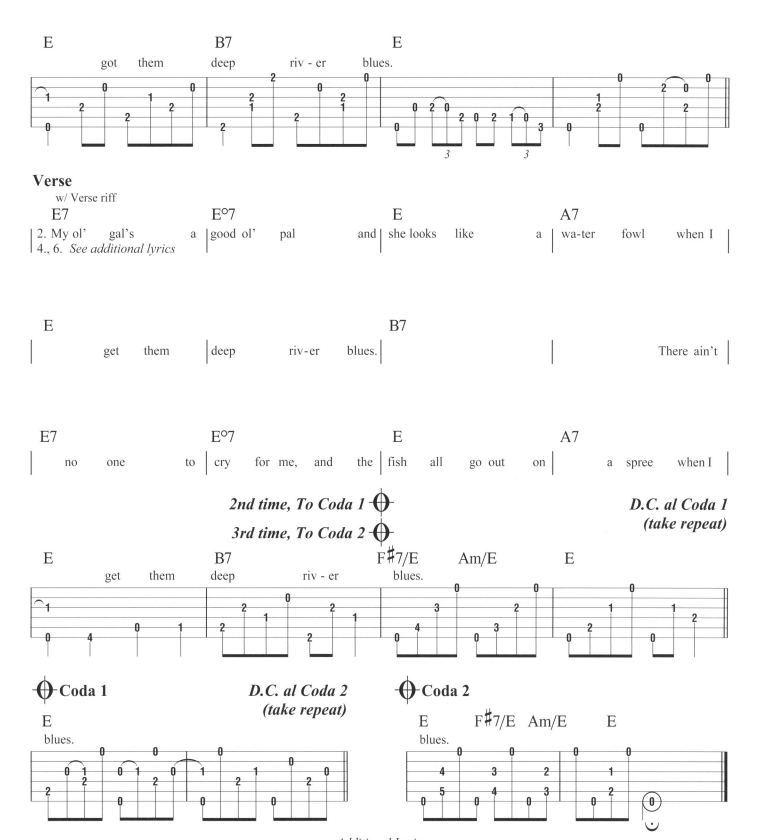

Verse

w/ Verse riff

2. My ol' gal's a good ol' pal and she looks like a wa-ter fowl when I
4., 6. *See additional lyrics*

get them deep riv-er blues. There ain't

no one to cry for me, and the fish all go out on a spree when I

2nd time, To Coda 1 ⊕

3rd time, To Coda 2 ⊕

D.C. al Coda 1
(take repeat)

get them deep riv-er blues.

⊕ **Coda 1**

blues.

D.C. al Coda 2
(take repeat)

⊕ **Coda 2**

blues.

Additional Lyrics

3. Give me back my old boat.
   I'm gonna sail if she'll float
   'Cause I got them deep river blues.
   I'm goin' back to Muscle Shoals.
   Times are better there, I'm told
   'Cause I got them deep river blues.

4., 6. Let it rain, let it pour.
   Let it rain a whole lot more
   'Cause I got them deep river blues.
   Let the rain drive right on,
   Let the waves sweep along
   'Cause I got them deep river blues.

5. If my boat sinks with me,
   I'll go down. Don't you see?
   'Cause I got them deep river blues.
   Now I'm gonna say goodbye
   And if I sink, just let me die
   'Cause I got them deep river blues.

Diamonds and Rust

Words and Music by Joan Baez

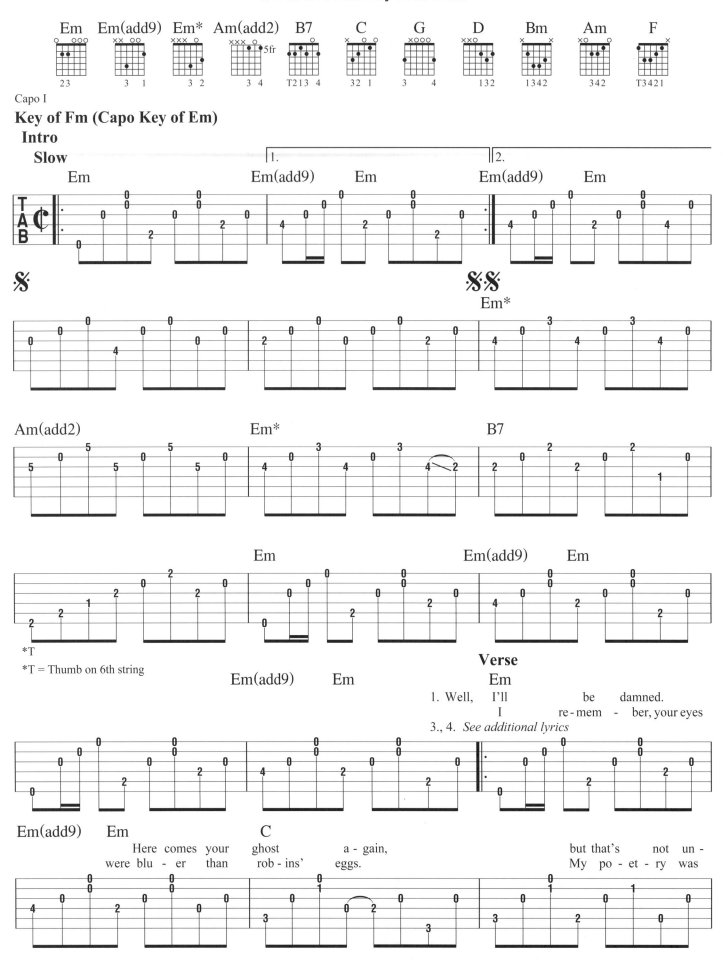

Capo I

Key of Fm (Capo Key of Em)

Intro

Slow

*T = Thumb on 6th string

Verse

1. Well,   I'll   be   damned.
   I   re - mem - ber, your eyes
3., 4. *See additional lyrics*

Here comes your ghost   a - gain,   but that's   not un -
were blu - er   than rob - ins' eggs.   My po - et - ry was

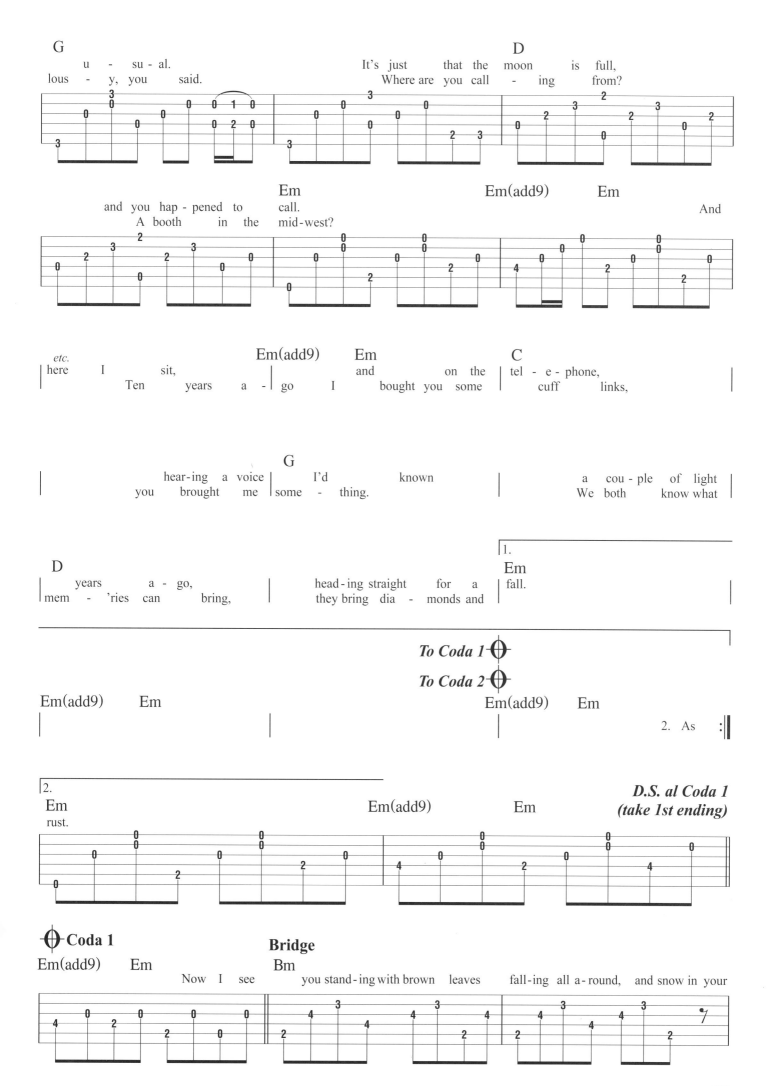

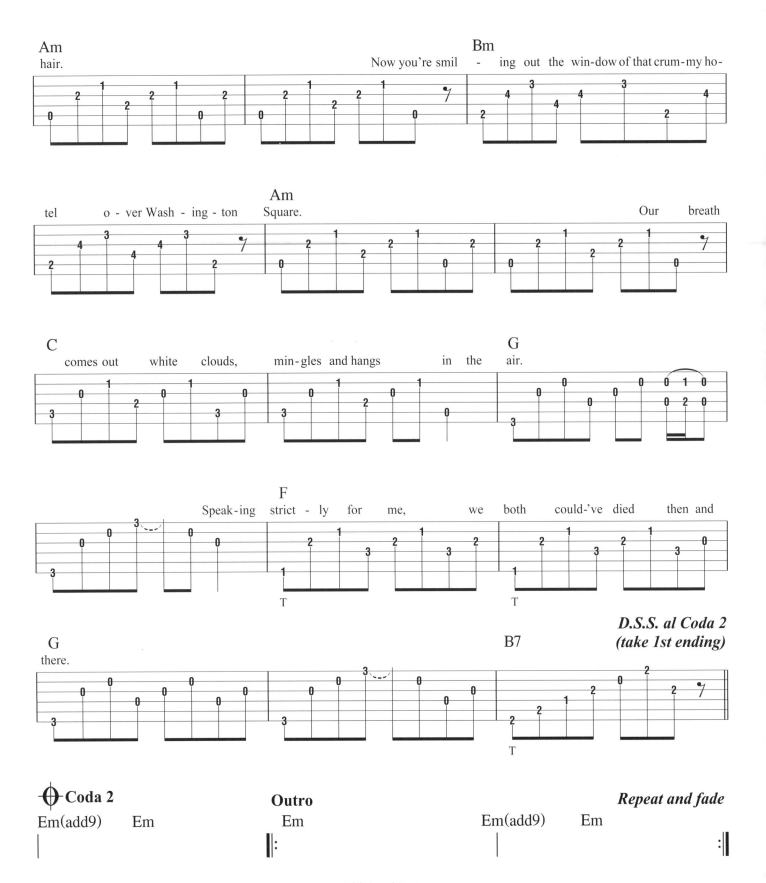

D.S.S. al Coda 2
(take 1st ending)

Φ **Coda 2**
Em(add9)   Em

Outro
Em

Repeat and fade
Em(add9)   Em

Additional Lyrics

3. Well, you burst on the scene
   Already a legend,
   The unwashed phenomenon,
   The original vagabond,
   You strayed into my arms.
   And there you stayed,
   Temporarily lost at sea.
   The madonna was yours for free.
   Yes, the girl on the half shell
   Could keep you unharmed.

4. Now, you're telling me
   You're not nostalgic,
   Then give me another word for it.
   You're so good with words
   And at keeping things vague.
   'Cause I need some of that vagueness now,
   It's all come back too clearly.
   Yes, I loved you dearly,
   And if you're offering me diamonds and rust,
   I've already paid.

Dust in the Wind

Words and Music by Kerry Livgren

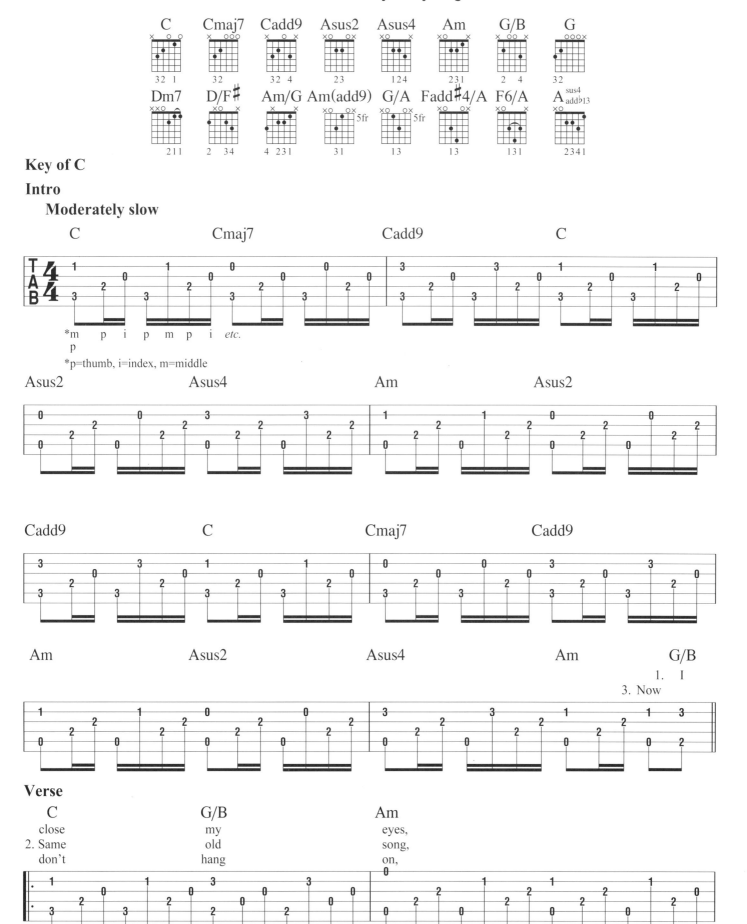

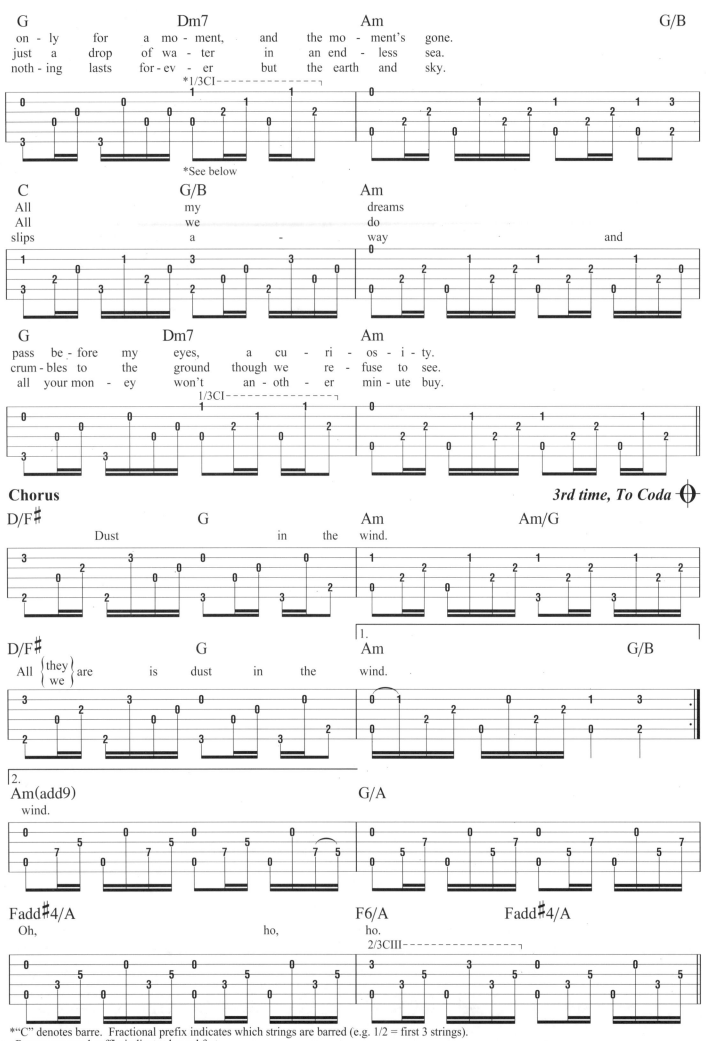

Chorus

3rd time, To Coda ⊕

*"C" denotes barre. Fractional prefix indicates which strings are barred (e.g. 1/2 = first 3 strings).
Roman numeral suffix indicates barred fret.

Instrumental Bridge

Am(add9)   G/A

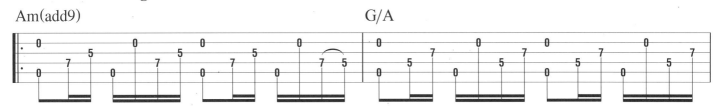

2nd time, D.C. al Coda

Fadd♯4/A   F6/A   Fadd♯4/A

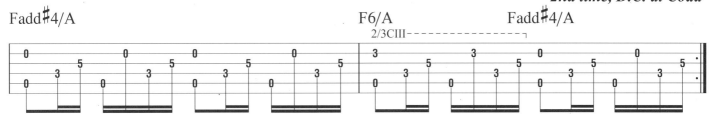

⊕ Coda

D/F♯   G   Am   Am/G

All we are   is dust in the wind.   (All we are is dust in the

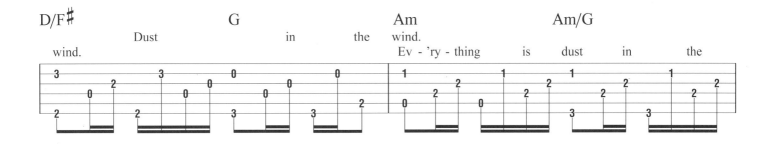

D/F♯   G   Am   Am/G

wind.   Dust   in the wind.   Ev - 'ry - thing is dust in the

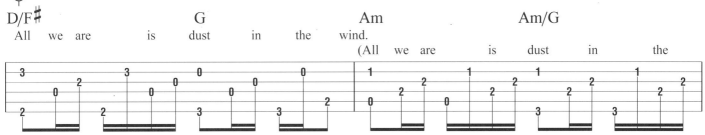

Outro

w/ Voc. ad lib. on repeats

D/F♯   G   Am   Asus2

Ev - 'ry - thing is dust in the wind.

wind.)

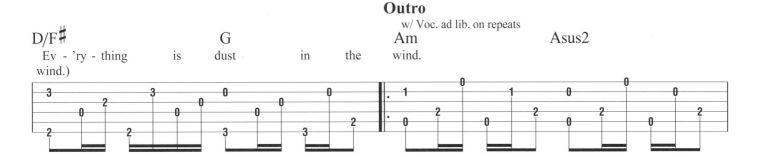

Repeat and fade

A$_{add♭13}^{sus4}$ Am   Asus2   A$_{add♭13}^{sus4}$

The   wind.

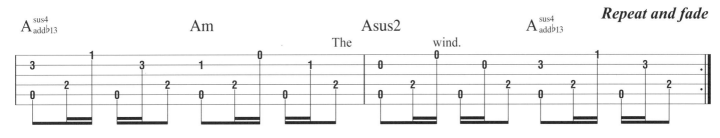

Don't Think Twice, It's All Right

Words and Music by Bob Dylan

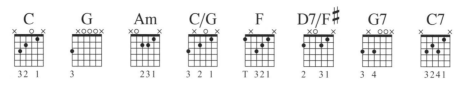

Capo IV

Key of E (Capo Key of C)

Intro

Moderately

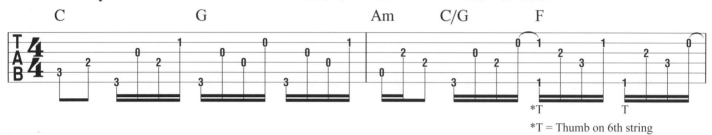

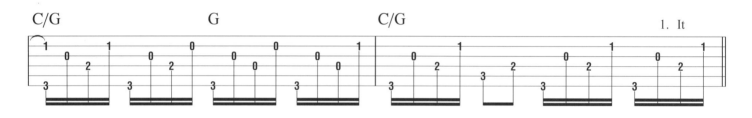

*T = Thumb on 6th string

1. It

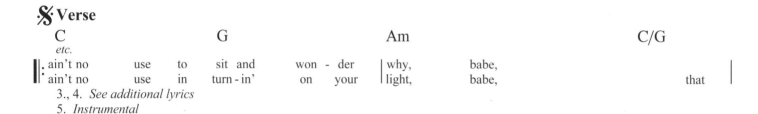

Verse

etc.

|: ain't no   use   to   sit and   won - der | why,   babe, | | that |
|: ain't no   use   in   turn - in'   on your | light,   babe, | | |

3., 4. *See additional lyrics*
5. *Instrumental*

F		C	G
it don't mat-ter an - y	how.		An' it
light I	nev - er	knowed.		An' it

C	G	Am	C/G
ain't no use to sit and won - der	why, babe,		
ain't no use in turn - in' on your	light, babe,		

D7/F♯	G	G7	
if you don't know by	now.		When your
I'm on the dark side of the	road.		Still I

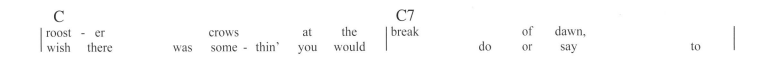

C							C7				
roost - er			crows	at	the	break		of	dawn,		
wish there		was	some - thin' you	would			do	or	say		to

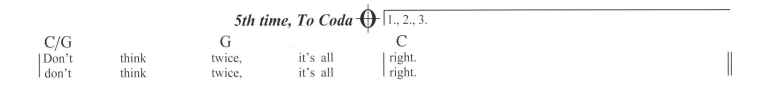

F						D7/F♯				
look	out	your	win - dow	and		I'll	be	gone.		
try	and		make	me	change my	mind	and	stay.		

C/G			G		Am	C/G	F	
You're	the	rea - son I'm		talk - in'	trav - 'lin'	on.		
We nev -	er	did too	much	talk - in' an - y - way.				So

5th time, To Coda ⊕ ⌐ 1., 2., 3.

C/G		G		C	
Don't	think	twice,	it's all	right.	
don't	think	twice,	it's all	right.	

Harmonica Solo

C	G	Am	C/G	F

⌐ 4.

C				C	
			2. It	right.	

D.S. al Coda

⊕ **Coda**

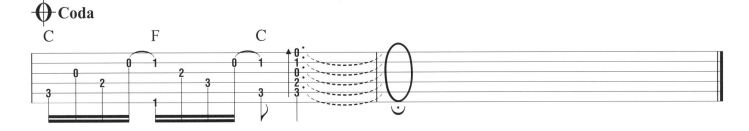

Additional Lyrics

3. It ain't no use in callin' out my name, gal,
Like you never did before.
It ain't no use in callin' out my name, gal,
I can't hear you anymore.
I'm a-thinkin' and a-wond'rin' all the way down the road
I once loved a woman, a child I'm told.
I give her my heart but she wanted my soul,
But don't think twice, it's all right.

4. I'm walkin' down that long, lonesome road, babe,
Where I'm bound, I can't tell.
But goodbye's too good a word, gal,
So I'll just say fare thee well.
I ain't sayin' you treated me unkind,
You could have done better but I don't mind.
You just kinda wasted my precious time.
But don't think twice, it's all right.

Embryonic Journey

Music by Jorma Kaukonen

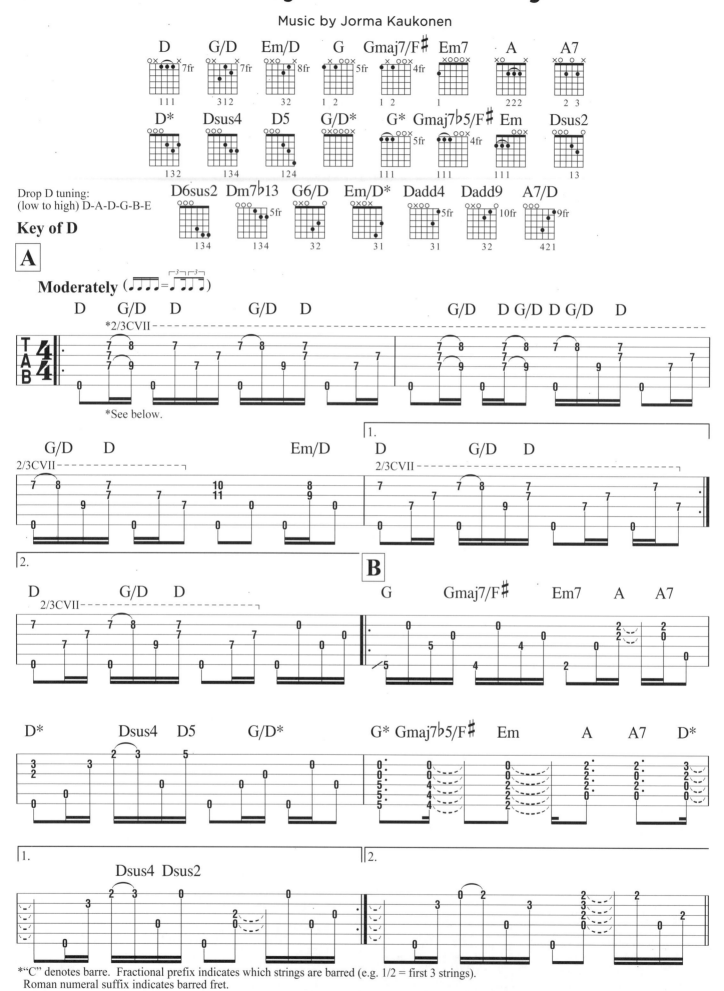

Drop D tuning:
(low to high) D-A-D-G-B-E

Key of D

*"C" denotes barre. Fractional prefix indicates which strings are barred (e.g. 1/2 = first 3 strings).
Roman numeral suffix indicates barred fret.

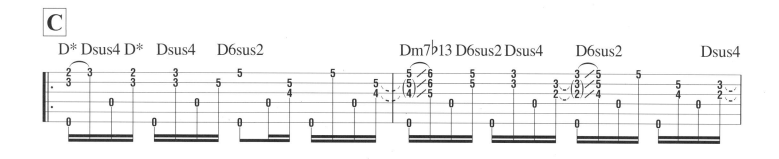

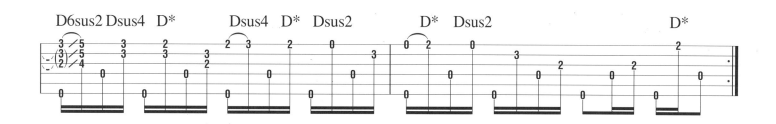

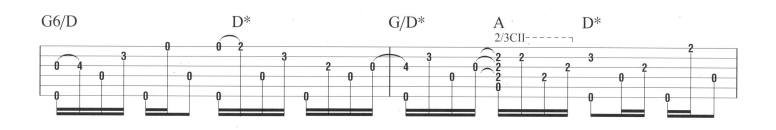

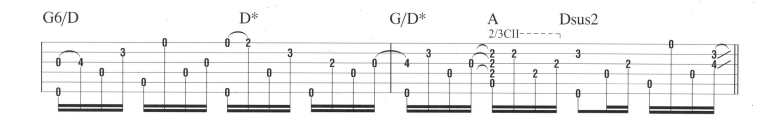

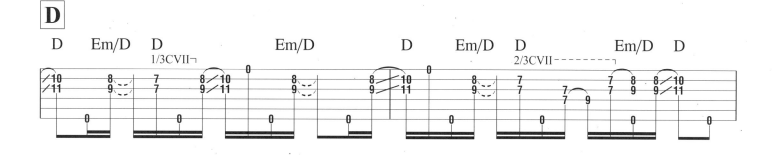

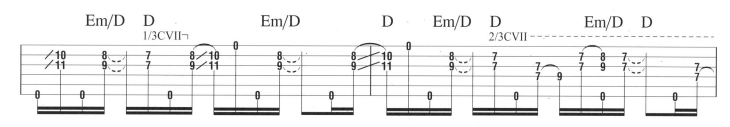

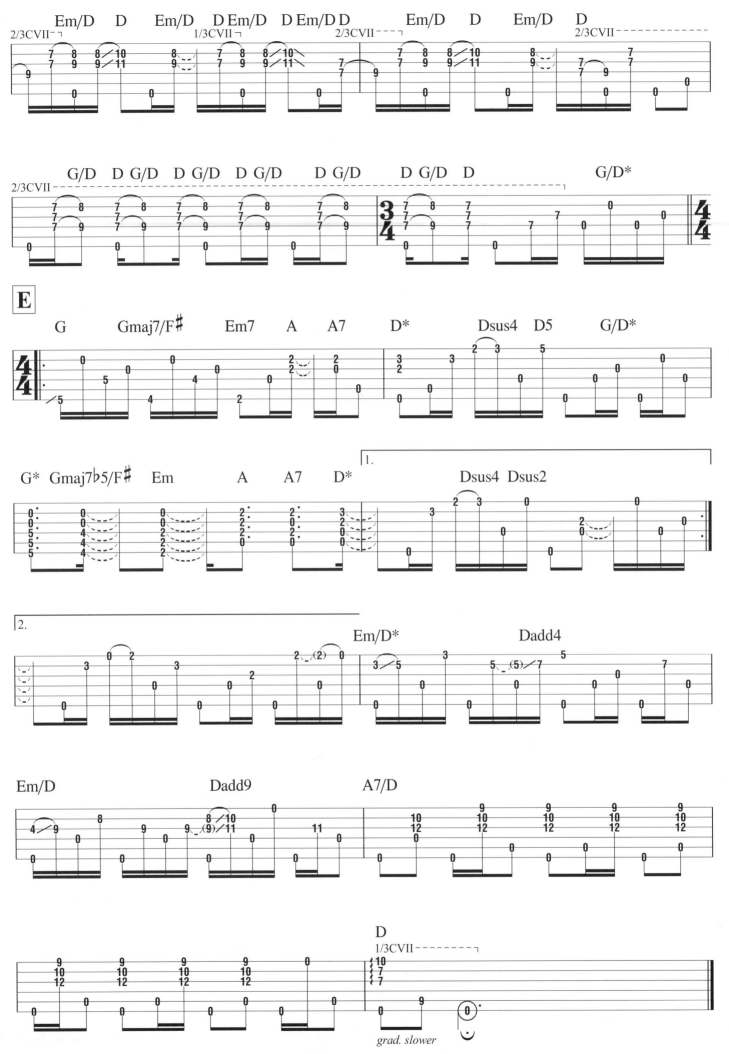

Hard Time Killing Floor Blues

Words and Music by Nehemiah "Skip" James

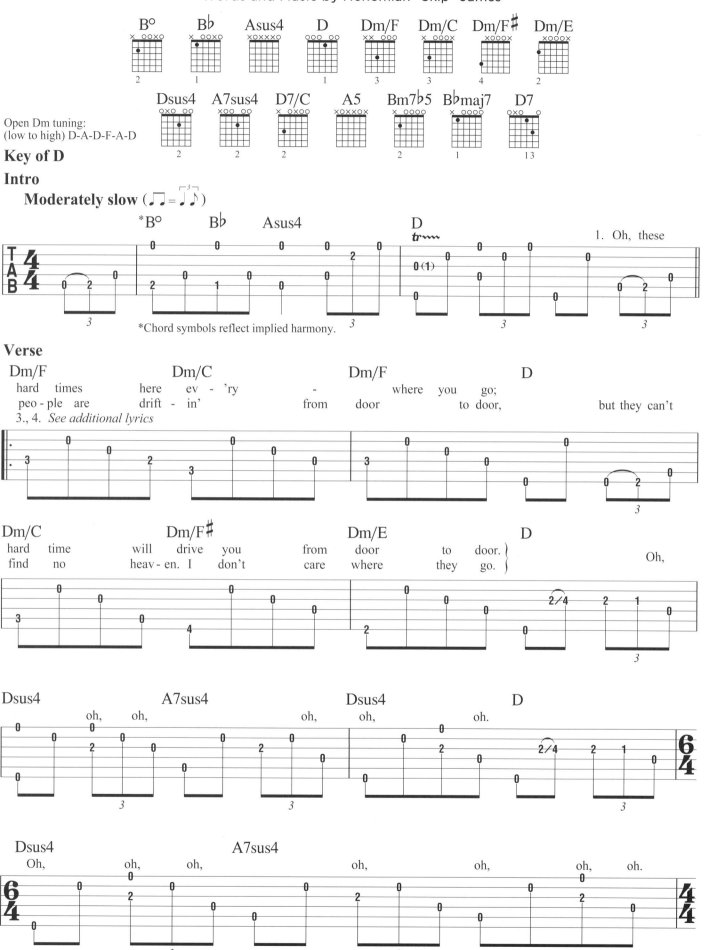

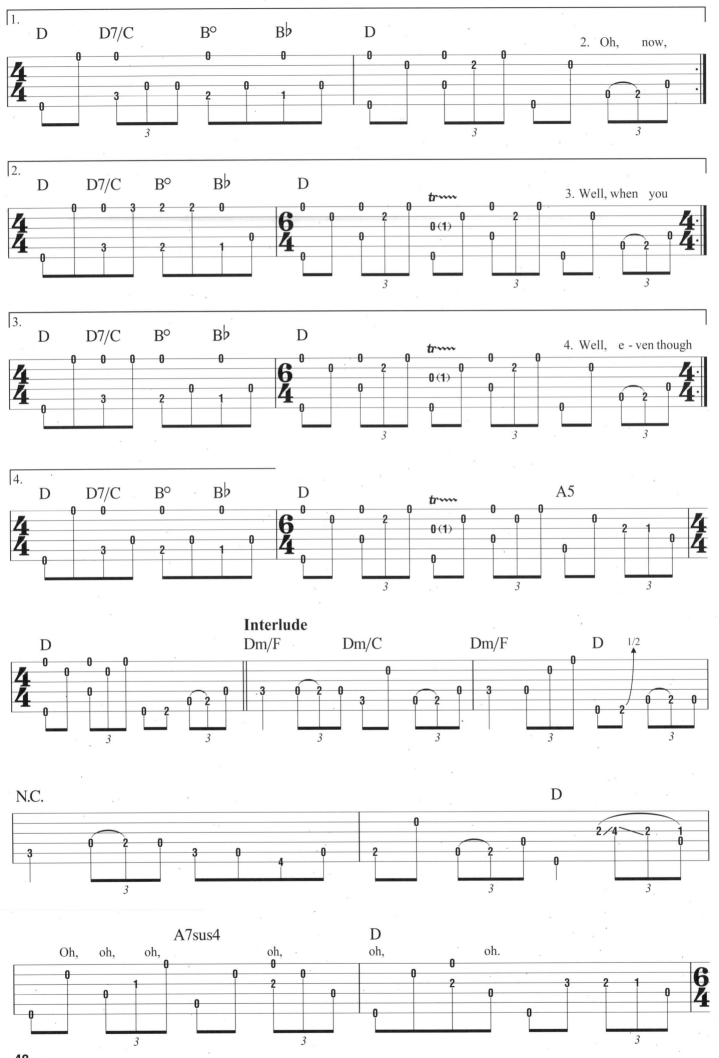

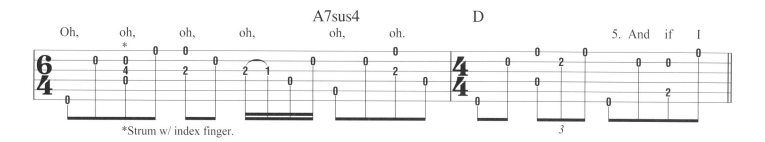

Verse

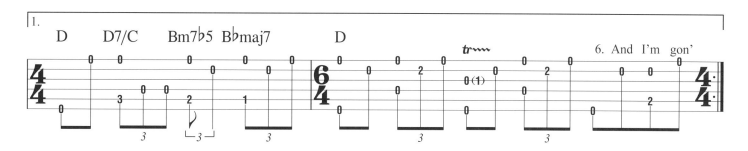

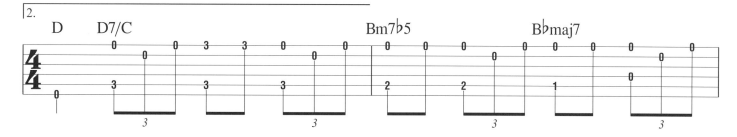

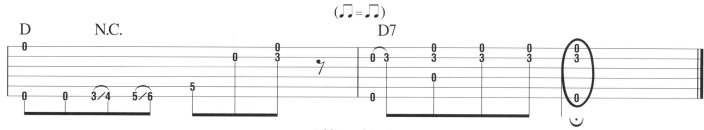

Additional Lyrics

3. Well, when you hear me sing this old lonesome song,
   You know these hard times can't last for very long.
   Oh...

4. Well, even though you say you had money, you better be sure.
   'Cause these hard times gonna drive you from door to door.
   Oh...

The Entertainer

By Scott Joplin
Arranged by John Knowles

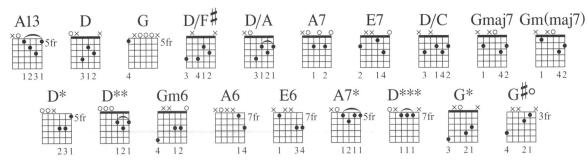

Drop D tuning:
(low to high) D-A-D-G-B-E

Key of D

 A

Moderately

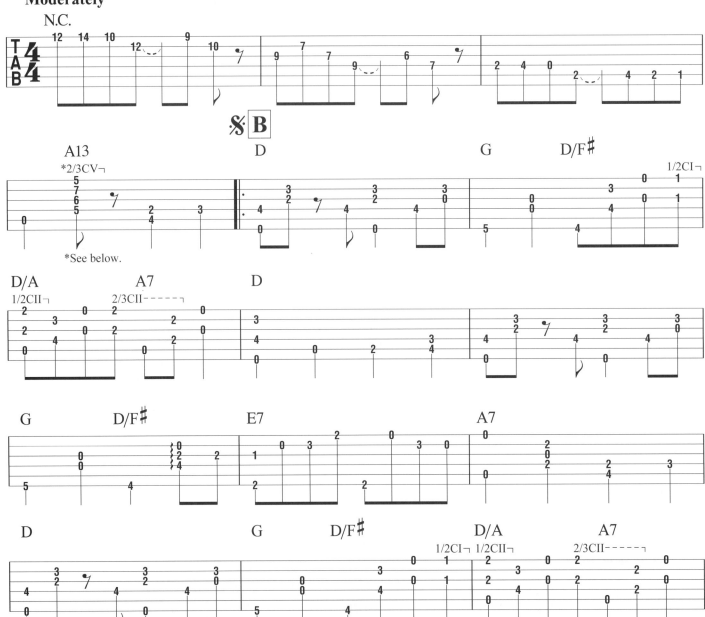

*"C" denotes barre. Fractional prefix indicates which strings are barred (e.g. 1/2 = first 3 strings).
Roman numeral suffix indicates barred fret.

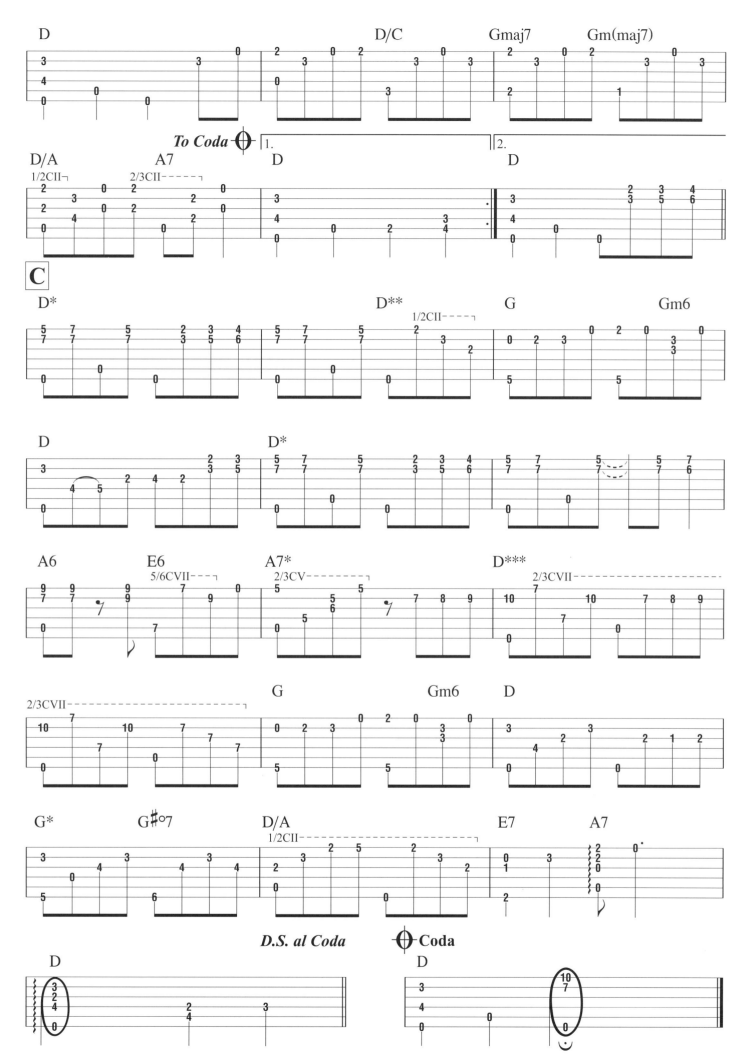

Falling Slowly

from the Motion Picture ONCE
Words and Music by Glen Hansard and Marketa Irglova

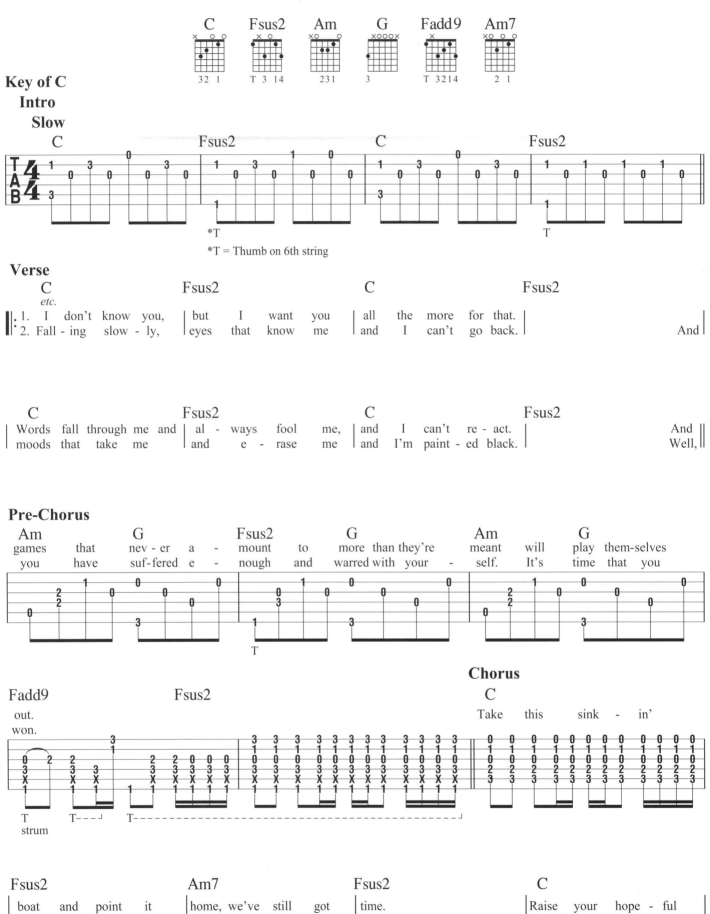

Key of C
Intro
Slow

*T = Thumb on 6th string

Verse

1. I don't know you, but I want you all the more for that. And
2. Fall - ing slow - ly, eyes that know me and I can't go back.

Words fall through me and al - ways fool me, and I can't re - act. And
moods that take me and e - rase me and I'm paint - ed black. Well,

Pre-Chorus

games that nev - er a - mount to more than they're meant will play them-selves
you have suf-fered e - nough and warred with your - self. It's time that you

Chorus

out.
won.

Take this sink - in'

boat and point it home, we've still got time. Raise your hope - ful

Fsus2   Am7   Fsus2   1.

voice, you have a | choice. {You'll make it / You've made it} now.   :||

2.

C   Fsus2   Am7

Fall - in' slow - ly, | sing your mel - o - | dy. I'll sing it

Fsus2   **Outro** C   Fsus2

loud.

Am7   Fsus2

| | | To come, |

| | a, pay the cost | too late. | |

| Now you're gone. | | |

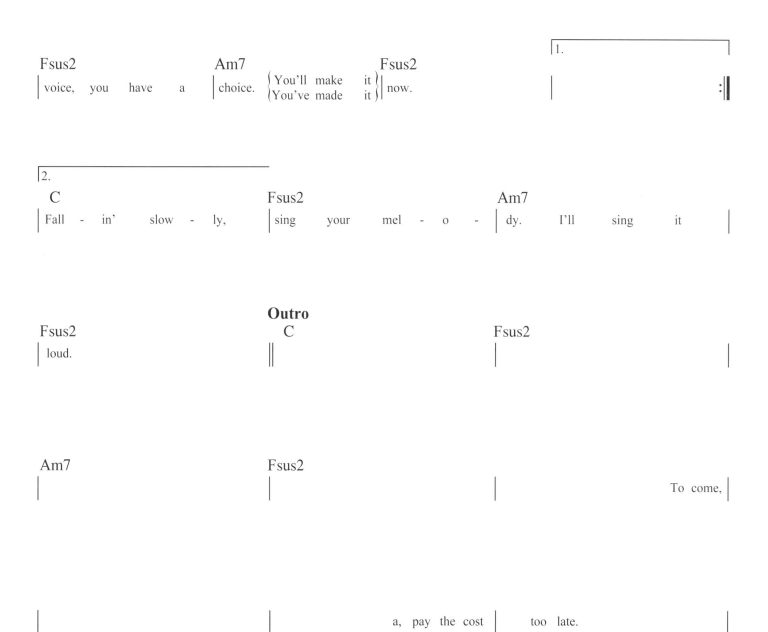

Fsus2

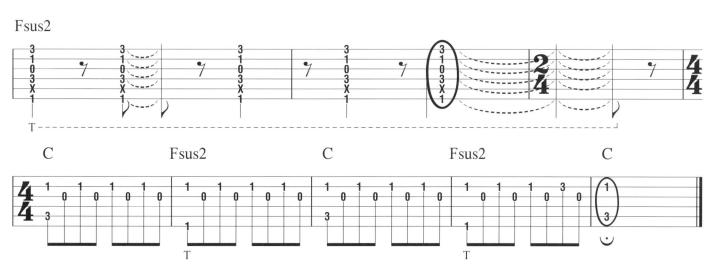

C   Fsus2   C   Fsus2   C

Fire and Rain

Words and Music by James Taylor

Capo III

Key of C
(Capo Key of A)

Intro

Moderately slow

Verse

1. Just yes - ter - day morn - in', they let me know you were gone.
   look down up - on me, Je - sus. you got to help me make a stand.
3. *See additional lyrics*

Su - zanne, the plans they made put an end to you.
You've just got to see me through an - oth - er day.

I walked out this morn - ing and I wrote down this song.
My bod - y's ach - ing and my time is at hand.

I just can't re - mem - ber who to send it to.
I won't make it an - y oth - er way.

*"C" denotes barre. Fractional prefix indicates which strings are barred (e.g. 1/2 = first 3 strings).
Roman numeral suffix indicates barred fret.

Chorus

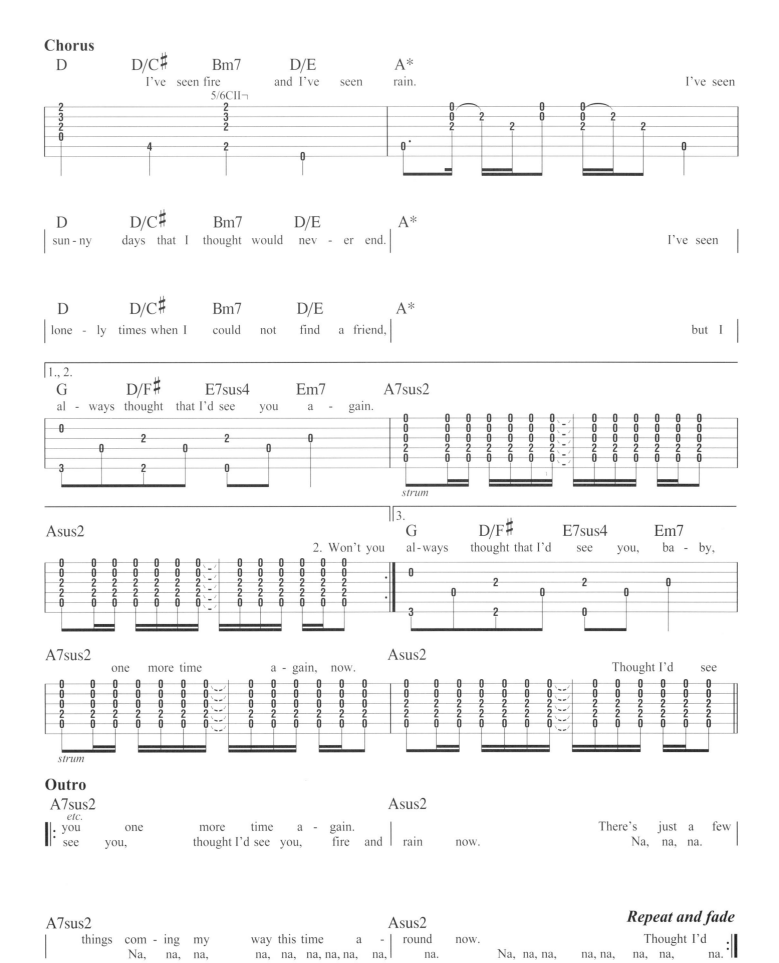

Additional Lyrics

3. Been walking my mind to an easy time, my back turned towards the sun.
Lord knows when the cold wind blows, it'll turn your head around.
Well, there's hours of time on the telephone line to talk about things to come,
Sweet dreams and flying machines in pieces on the ground.

Forever

Words and Music by Ben Harper

Key of C
Intro
Moderately slow

*T = Thumb on 6th string

Verse

talk-in' 'bout a year,   no,   not three or   four.   I don't
2., 4. *See additional lyrics*
3. *Instrumental*

want that kind of for - ev - er   in my   life   an - y - more.   For-

ev - er al - ways   seems   to be a-round   when it   be - gins,   but for-

ev - er   nev - er   seems   to be a - round   when it ends.   So give me your

Chorus

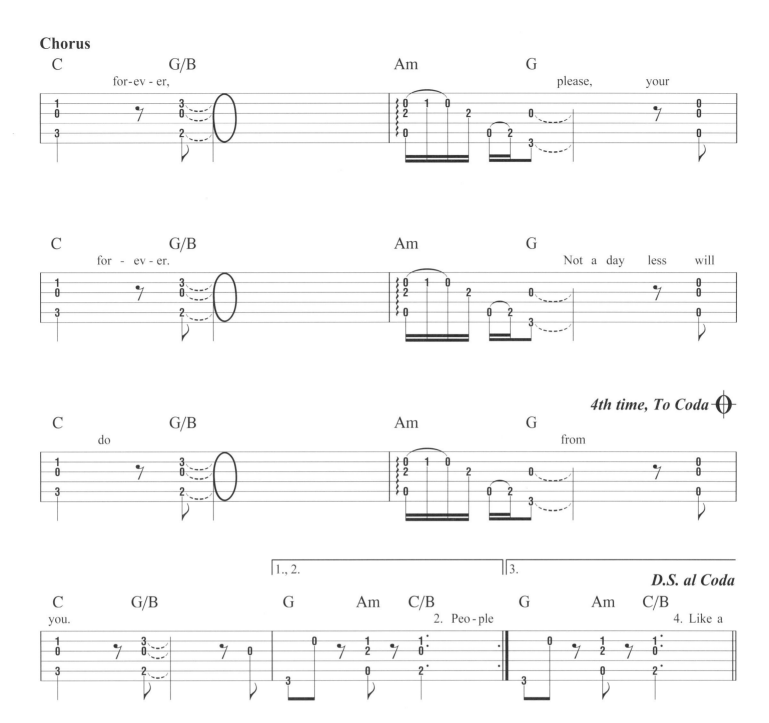

4th time, To Coda ⊕

D.S. al Coda

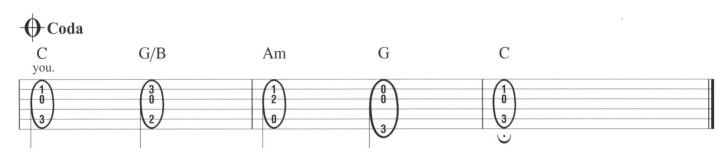

⊕ **Coda**

Additional Lyrics

2. People spend so much time ev'ry single day
   Running 'round all over town giving their forever away.
   But no, not me, I won't let my forever roam,
   And now I hope I can find my forever a home.

4. Like a handless clock with numbers, an infinite of time,
   No, not the forever found only in the mind.
   Forever always seems to be around when things begin,
   But forever never seems to be around when things end.

Freight Train

Words and Music by Elizabeth Cotten

Tune down 1 step:
(low to high) D-G-C-F-A-D

Key of C

Intro

Moderately, in 2

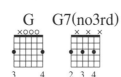

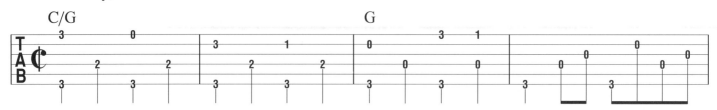

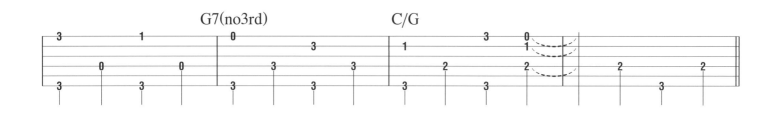

*T = Thumb on 6th string

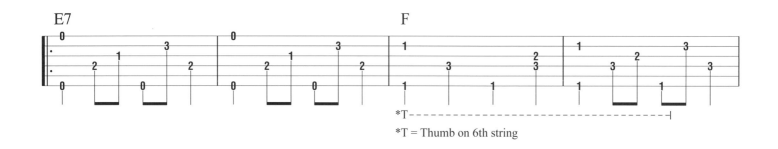

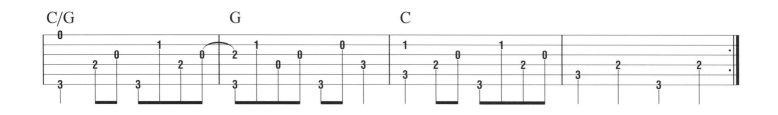

Verse

C/G   G

etc.

1. Freight   train, | freight   train | run   so   fast.
2. When   I   am | dead   and | in   my   grave,
3., 4. *See additional lyrics*
5. *Instrumental*

G7(no3rd)			C/G		
Freight	train,	freight	train	run	so fast.
	no more	good	time	here	I pray.

E7			F		
Please	don't	tell	what	train	I'm on. They won't
Place	the stones		at my	head	and feet and tell 'em all

C/G		G		C	
know	what	route	I've	gone.	
	that I'm	gone	to	sleep.	

E7   F

C/G   G   1. - 4.   C

5.
C

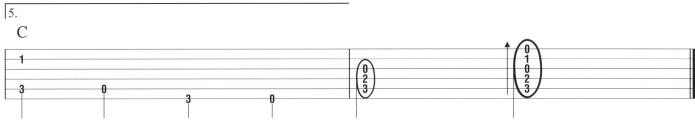

Additional Lyrics

3. When I die, Lord, bury me deep
   Way down on old Chestnut Street
   So I can hear old number nine
   As she come rollin' by.

4. When I die, Lord, bury me deep
   Way down on old Chestnut Street.
   Place the stones at my head and feet
   And tell 'em all that I'm gone to sleep.

From the Morning

Words and Music by Nick Drake

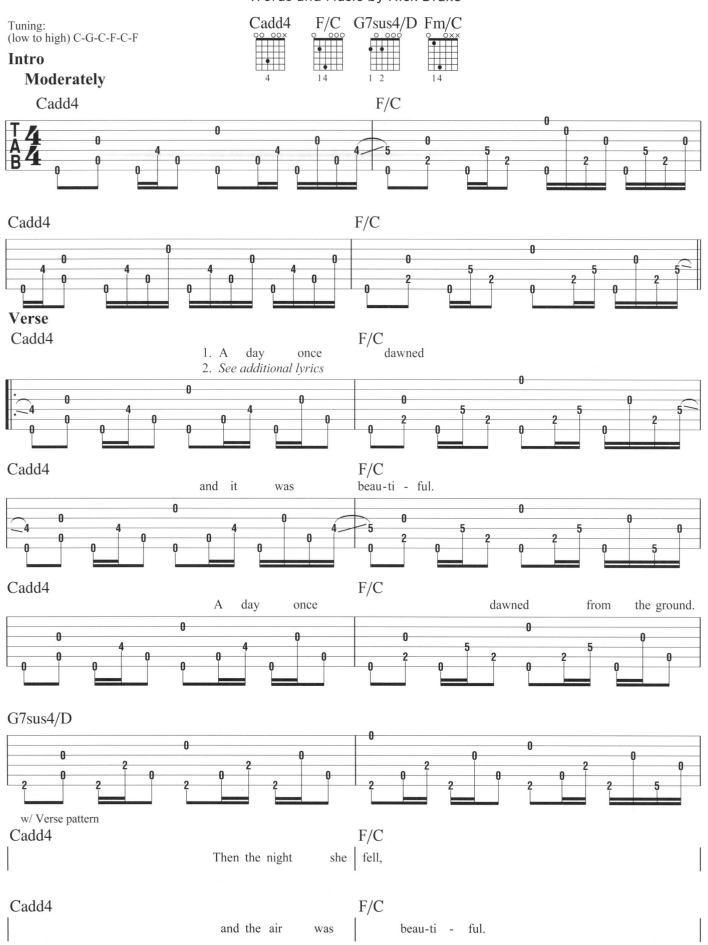

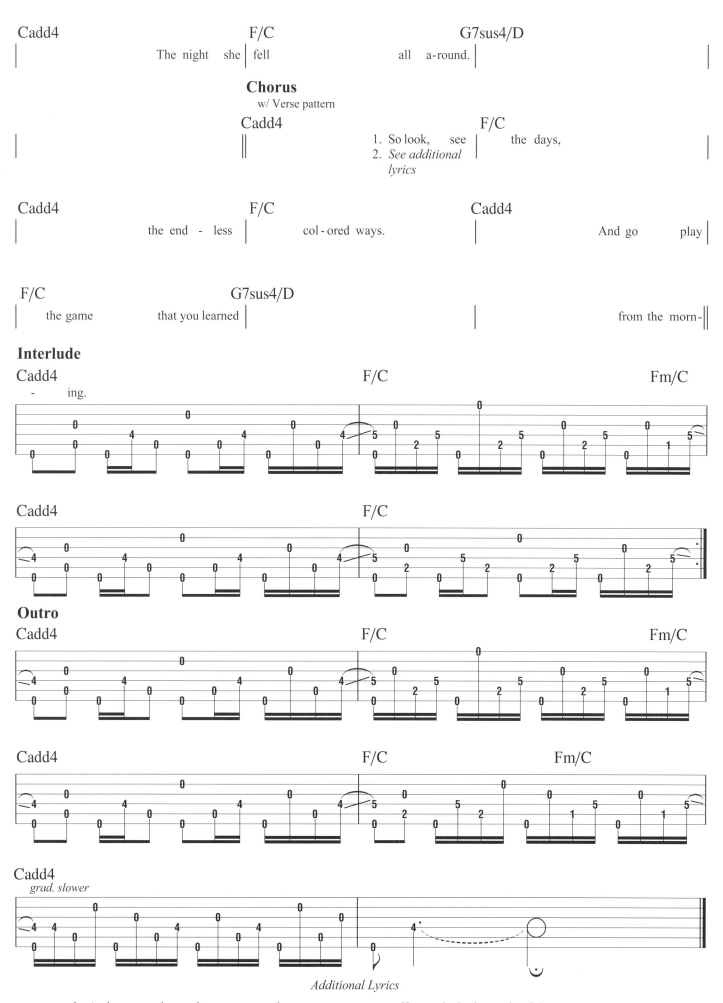

| Cadd4 | | F/C | | G7sus4/D |
| The night she | fell | | all a-round. | |

Chorus
w/ Verse pattern

	Cadd4		F/C
		1. So look, see	the days,
		2. *See additional*	
		lyrics	

| Cadd4 | | F/C | | Cadd4 |
| the end - less | | col - ored ways. | And go | play |

| F/C | | G7sus4/D | | |
| the game | that you learned | | from the morn- |

Interlude

Cadd4   F/C   Fm/C

Cadd4   F/C

- ing.

Outro

Cadd4   F/C   Fm/C

Cadd4   F/C   Fm/C

Cadd4
grad. slower

Additional Lyrics

2. And now we rise, and we are everywhere.
And now we rise from the ground.
And see she flies, and she is everywhere.
See she flies all around.

Chorus So look, see the sights,
The endless summer nights.
And go play the game that you learned
From the morning.

Going to California

Words and Music by Jimmy Page and Robert Plant

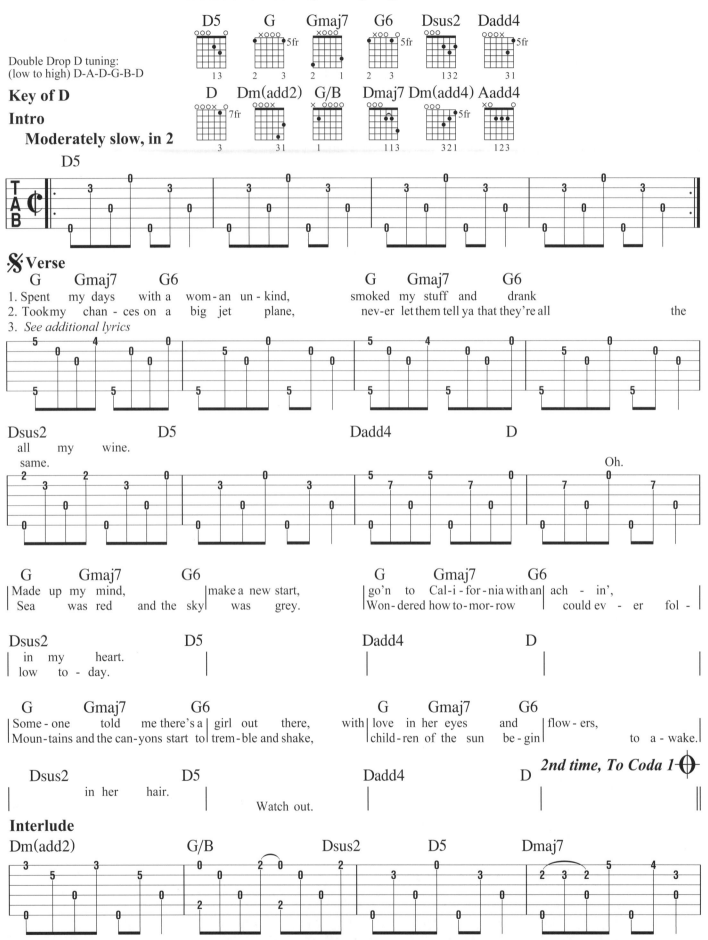

Double Drop D tuning:
(low to high) D-A-D-G-B-D

Key of D

Intro

Moderately slow, in 2

§ **Verse**

1. Spent my days with a wom-an un-kind, smoked my stuff and drank all my wine.
2. Took my chan-ces on a big jet plane, nev-er let them tell ya that they're all the same.
3. *See additional lyrics*

Oh.

Made up my mind, make a new start, go'n to Cal-i-for-nia with an ach-in',
Sea was red and the sky was grey. Won-dered how to-mor-row could ev - er fol -

in my heart.
low to - day.

Some - one told me there's a girl out there, with love in her eyes and flow - ers,
Moun-tains and the can-yons start to trem-ble and shake, child-ren of the sun be-gin to a-wake.

in her hair.
Watch out.

2nd time, To Coda 1

Interlude

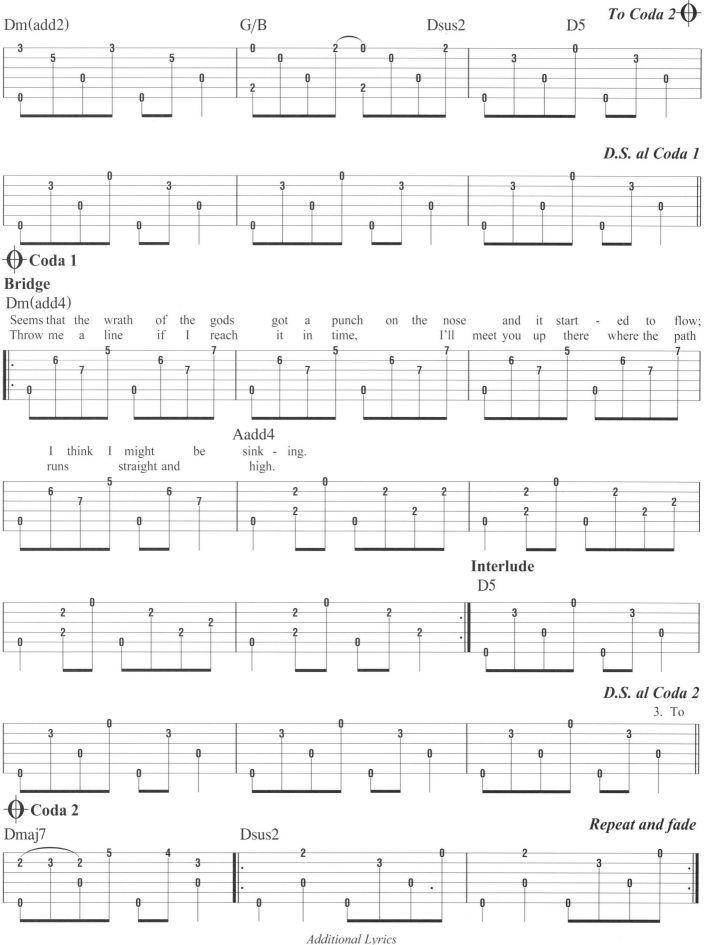

To Coda 2

D.S. al Coda 1

D.S. al Coda 2

Coda 1

Bridge

Seems that the wrath of the gods got a punch on the nose and it start - ed to flow;
Throw me a line if I reach it in time, I'll meet you up there where the path

I think I might be sink - ing.
runs straight and high.

Interlude

3. To

Coda 2

Repeat and fade

Additional Lyrics

3. To find a queen without a king,
They say she plays guitar and cries and sings. La, la, la, la.
Ride a white mare in the footsteps of dawn.
Tryin' to find a woman who's never, never, never been born.
Standin' on a hill in the mountain of dreams,
Tellin' myself it's not as hard, hard, hard as it seems.

Greensleeves

Traditional
Arrangement by Rod Stewart and Jeff Beck

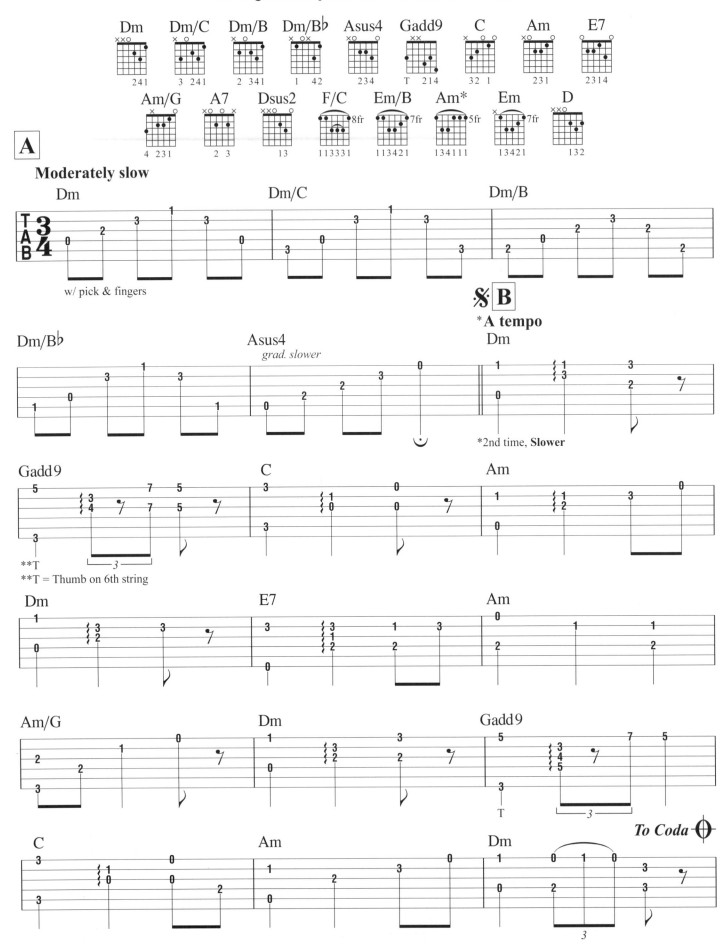

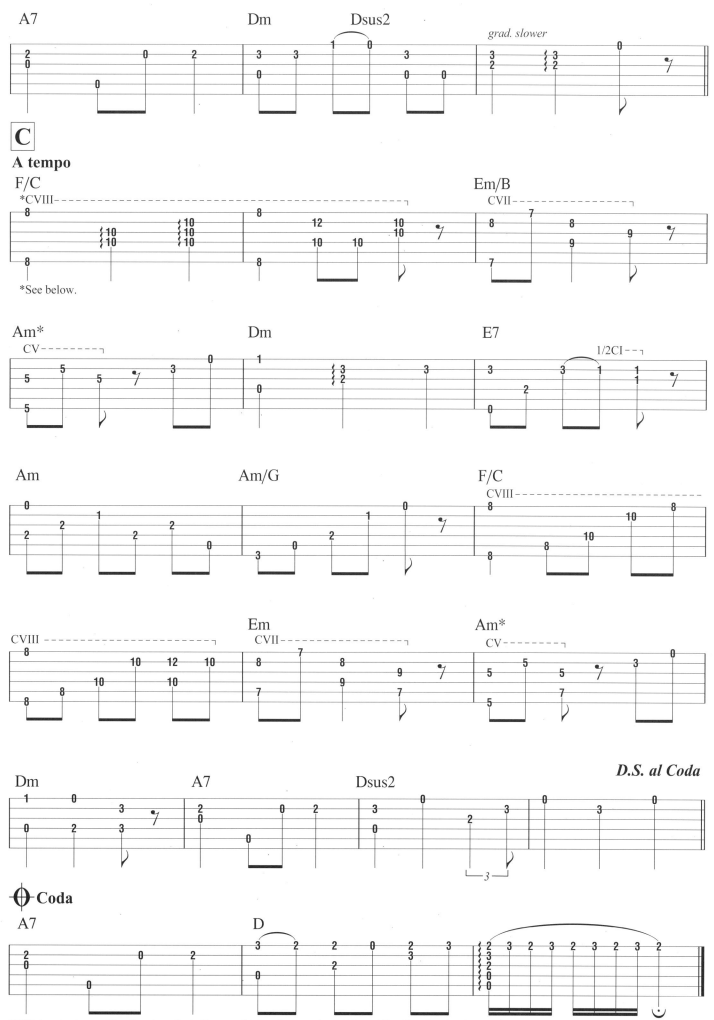

*"C" denotes barre. Fractional prefix indicates which strings are barred (e.g. 1/2 = first 3 strings).
 Roman numeral suffix indicates barred fret.

Hell Hound on My Trail

Words and Music by Robert Johnson

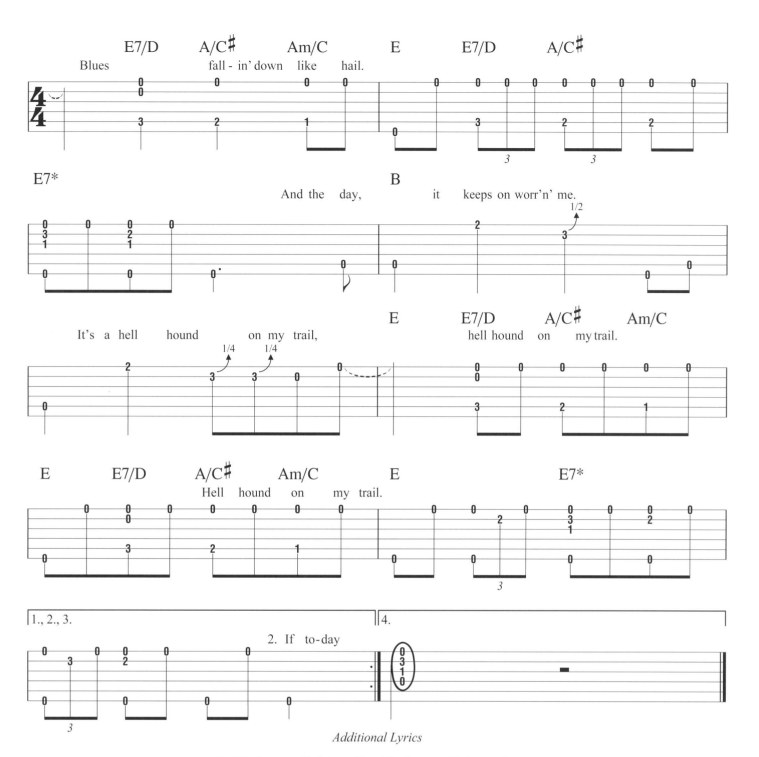

Additional Lyrics

2. If today was Christmas Eve, if today was Christmas Eve
   And tomorrow was Christmas Day,
   If today was Christmas Eve and tomorrow was Christmas Day,
   Spoken: *Aw, wouldn't we have a time, baby?*
   All I would need, my little sweet rider: just to pass the time away,
   Huh, huh, to pass the time away.

3. You sprinkled hot foot powder, mm, around my door,
   All around my door.
   You sprinkled hot foot powder all around your daddy's door,
   Hm, hm, hm.
   It keep me with a ramblin' mind, rider, ev'ry old place I go,
   Ev'ry old place I go.

4. I can tell the wind is risin', the leaves tremblin' on the tree,
   Tremblin' on the tree.
   I can tell the wind is risin', leaves tremblin' on the tree,
   Hm, hm, hm.
   All I need's my little sweet woman and to keep my company,
   Hey, my company.

Hello in There

Words and Music by John Prine

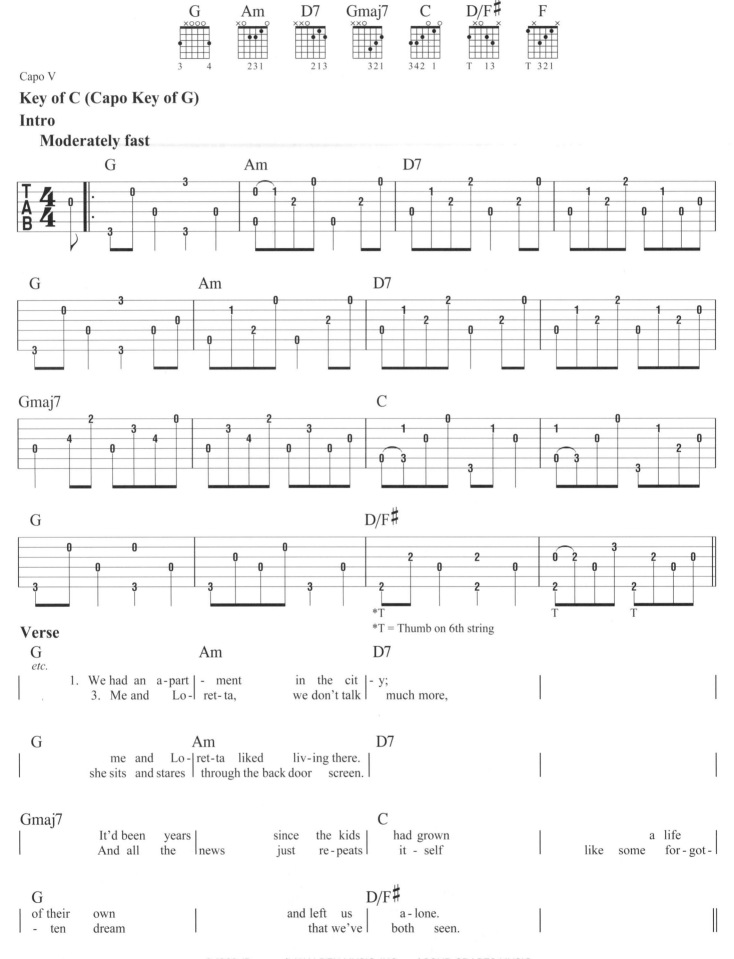

Capo V

Key of C (Capo Key of G)

Intro

Moderately fast

*T = Thumb on 6th string

Verse

G   Am   D7

etc.

1. We had an a-part- ment   in the cit - y;
3. Me and Lo- ret-ta,   we don't talk   much more,

G   Am   D7

me and Lo- ret-ta liked   liv-ing there.
she sits and stares through the back door screen.

Gmaj7   C

It'd been years since the kids had grown   a life
And all the news just re-peats it - self   like some for-got-

G   D/F#

of their own   and left us   a-lone.
- ten dream   that we've   both seen.

𝄋 Verse

G		Am		D7	
	2. John and Lin	- da	live in O	- ma - ha,	
	4. Some - day I'll	go and	call up Ru -	dy,	
	5. *See additional lyrics*				

G		Am		D7	
	and Joe is some	- where on the	road.		
	we worked to-geth	- er at the fac -	to - ry.		

Gmaj7				C	
	We lost Da	- vy	in the Ko -	re - an War,	and I still don't
	But what could I say		if he asks,	"What's new?"	"Noth - ing, what's

3rd time, To Coda ⊕

G			D/F♯	
know what for."		Don't mat-ter an	- y- more.	
with you?"		Noth-ing much	to do.	

Chorus

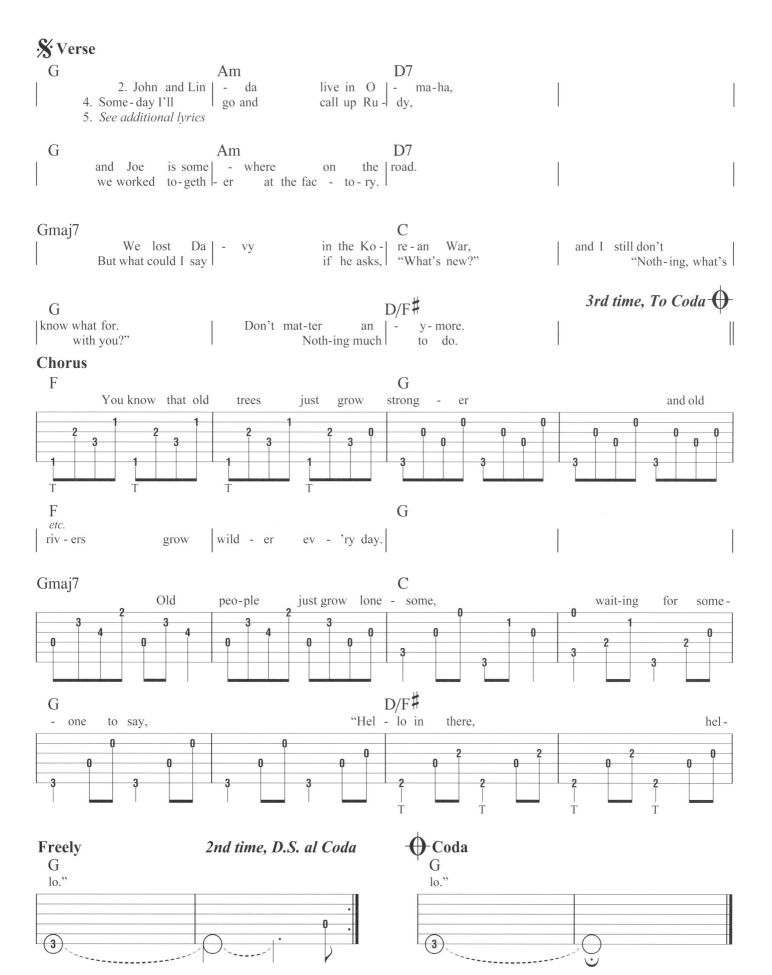

F — You know that old trees just grow strong - er and old

G

F *etc.* — riv - ers grow wild - er ev - 'ry day.

G

Gmaj7 — Old peo-ple just grow lone - some, wait-ing for some-

C

G — one to say, "Hel - lo in there, hel-

D/F♯

Freely

2nd time, D.S. al Coda

⊕ Coda

G lo."

G lo."

Additional Lyrics

5. So if you're walking down the street sometime
   And spot some hollow, ancient eyes,
   Please don't just pass 'em by and stare
   As if you didn't care.
   Say, "Hello in there, hello."

Helplessly Hoping

Words and Music by Stephen Stills

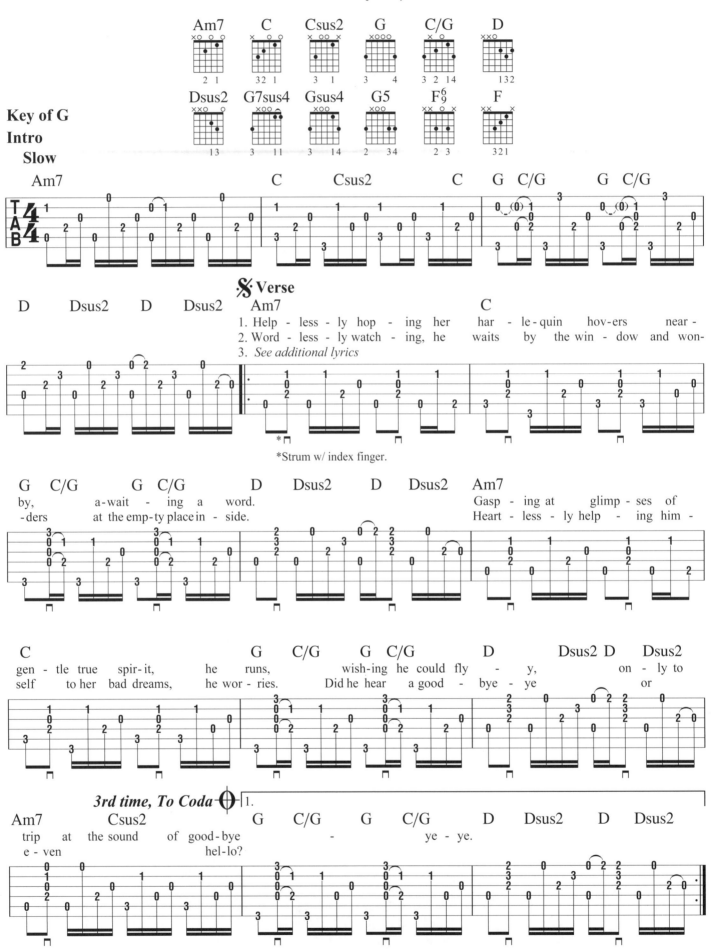

2.

Chorus

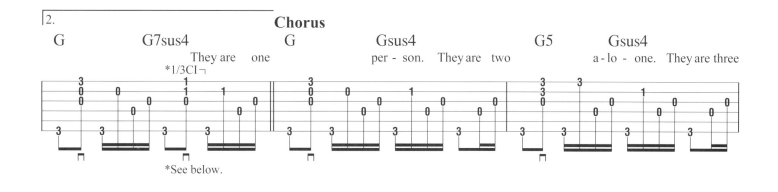

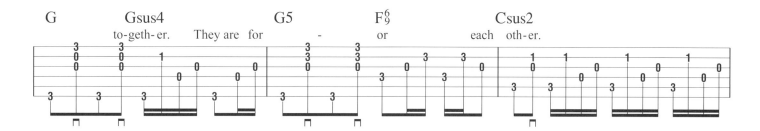

D.S. al Coda 〇 **Coda**

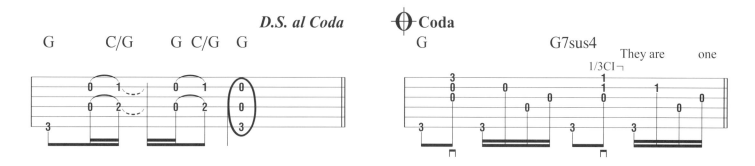

Outro-Chorus

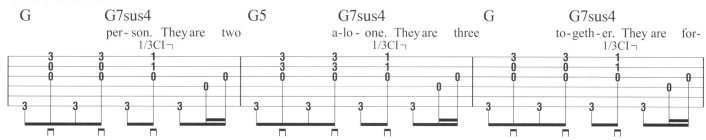

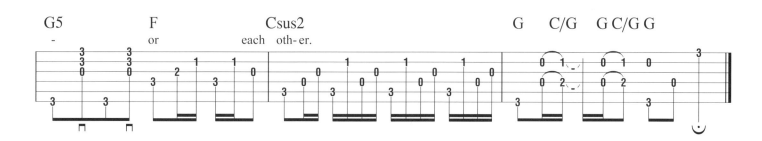

Additional Lyrics

3. Stand by the stairway, you'll see something certain to tell you
Confusion has its cost.
Love isn't lying, it's loose in a lady who lingers,
Saying she is lost and choking on hello.

*"C" denotes barre. Fractional prefix indicates which strings are barred (e.g. 1/2 = first 3 strings).
Roman numeral suffix indicates barred fret.

Horizons

By Anthony Banks, Phillip Collins, Peter Gabriel, Steve Hackett and Mike Rutherford

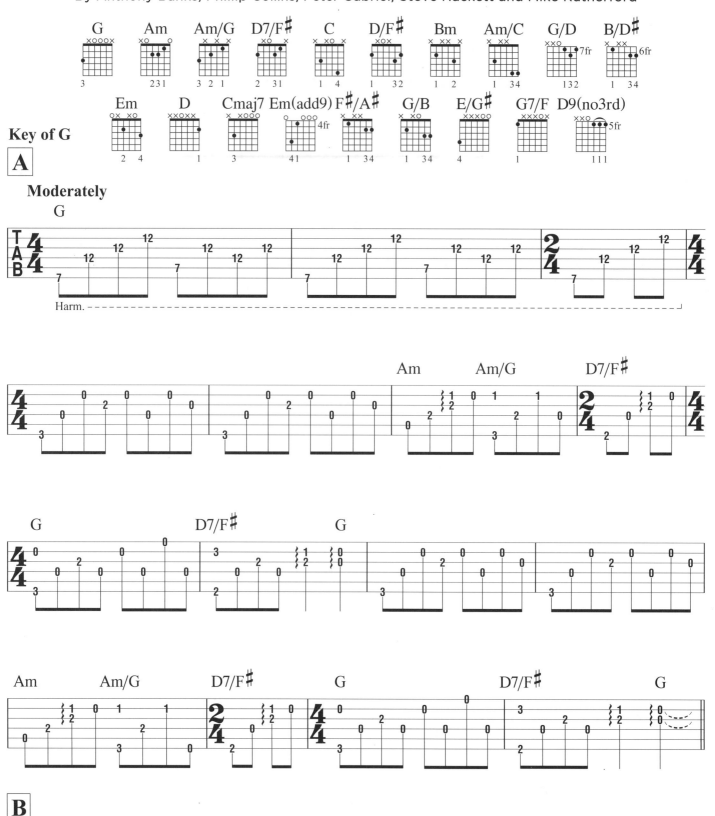

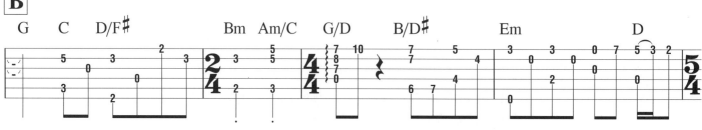

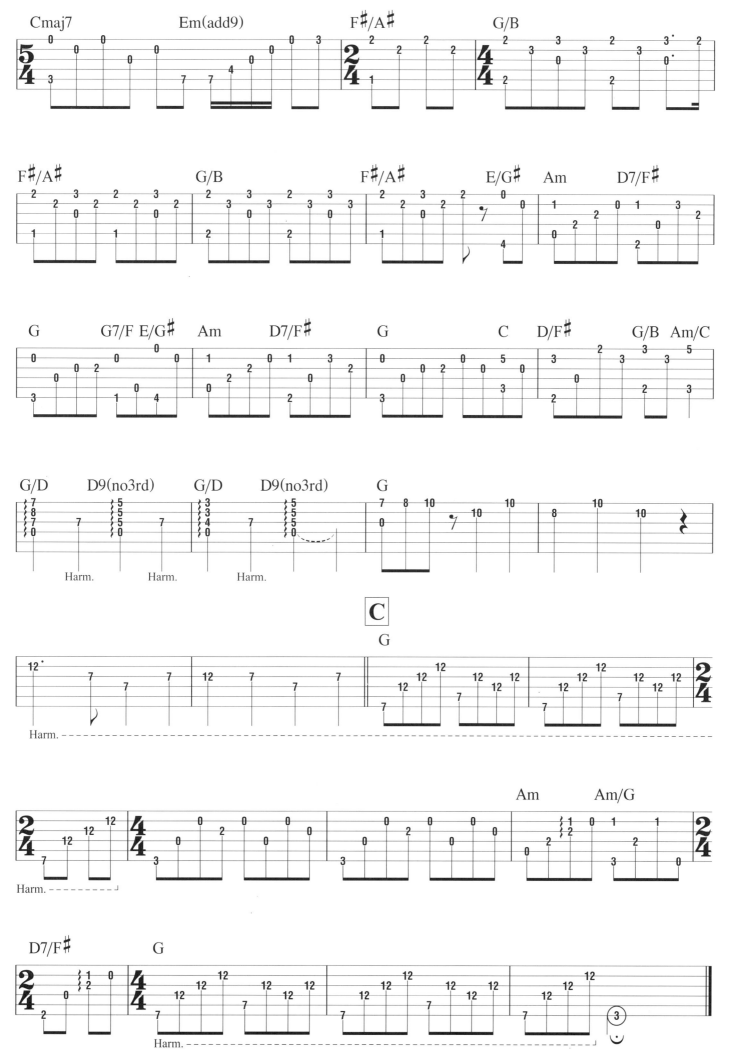

Is There Anybody Out There?

Words and Music by Roger Waters

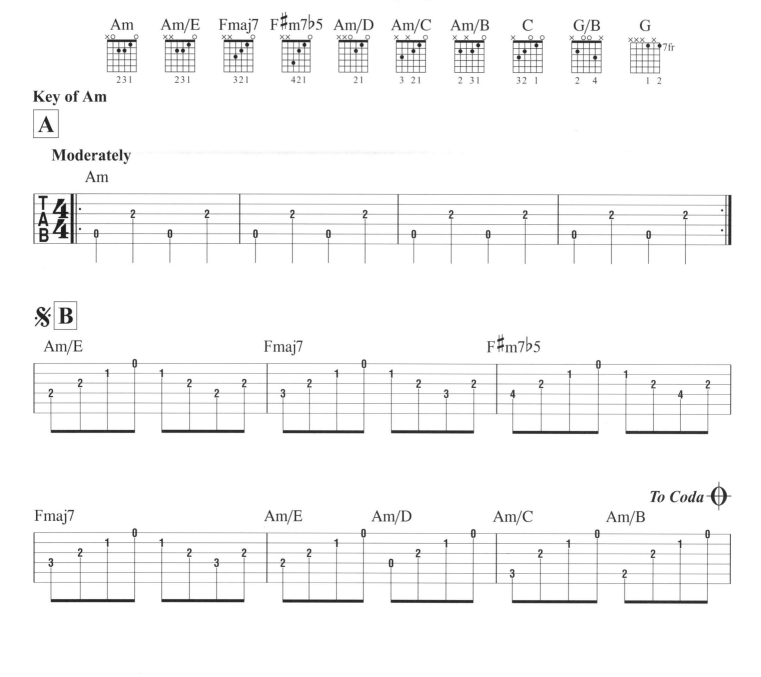

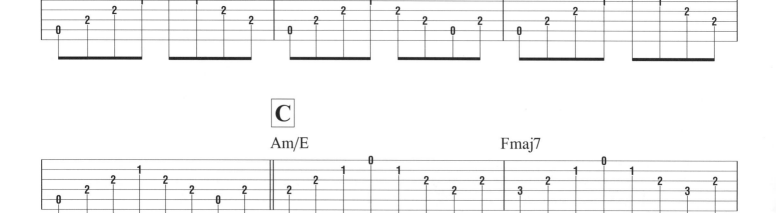

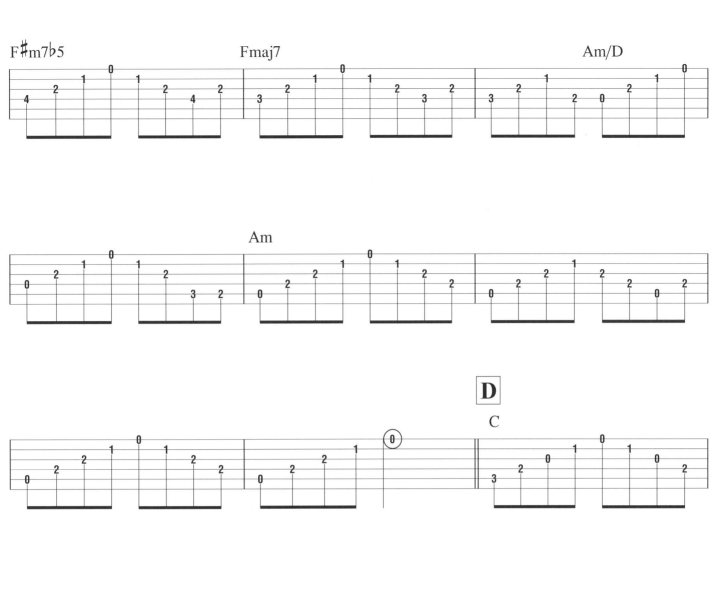

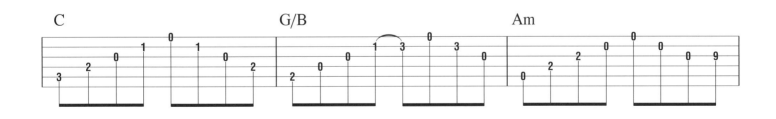

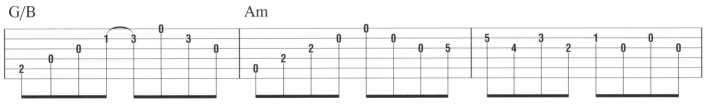

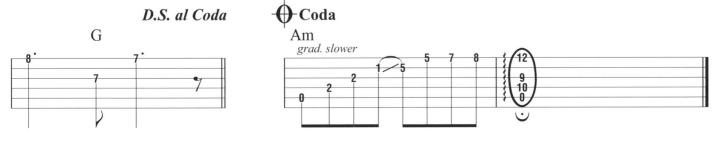

Jiffy Jam

Words and Music by Jerry Reed Hubbard

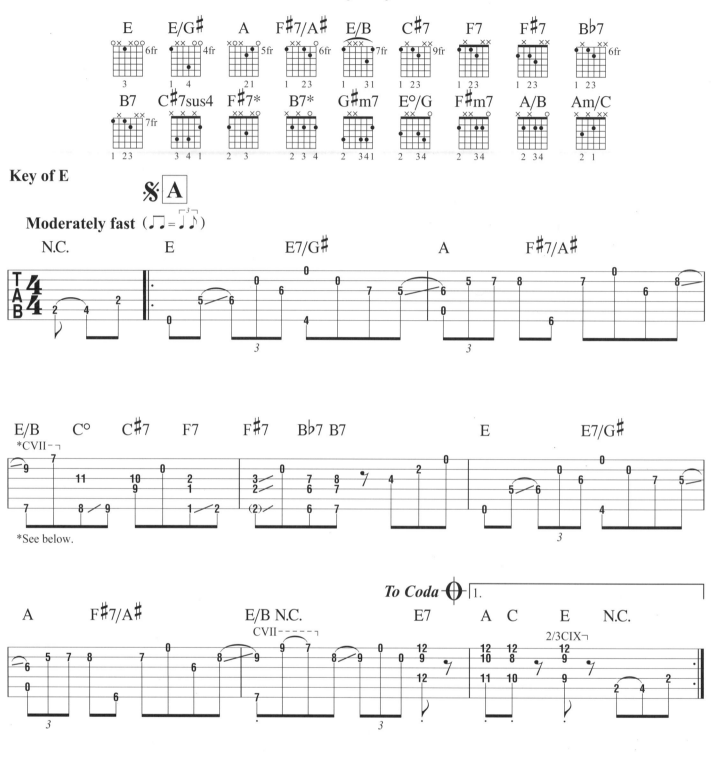

Key of E

Moderately fast

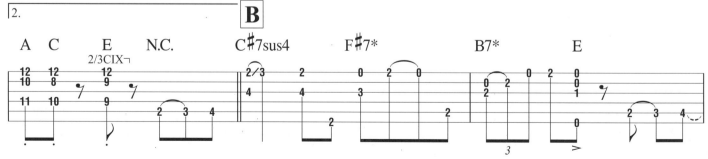

*"C" denotes barre. Fractional prefix indicates which strings are barred (e.g. 1/2 = first 3 strings).
Roman numeral suffix indicates barred fret.

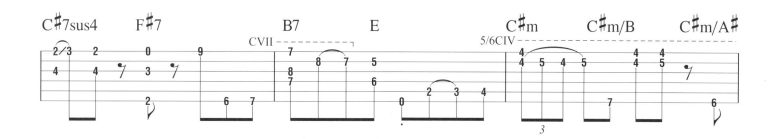

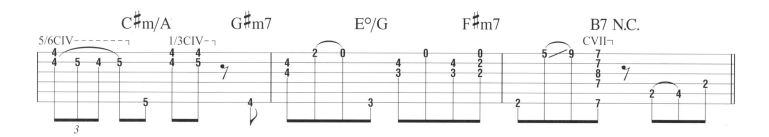

C

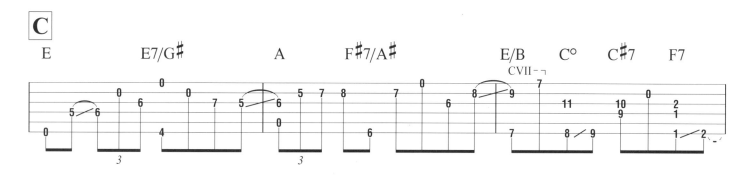

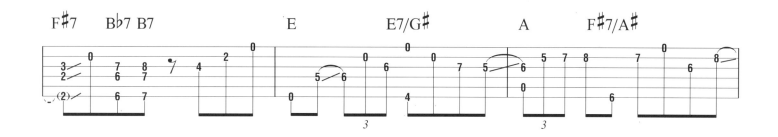

D.S. al Coda

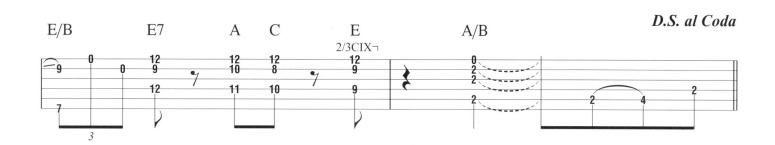

⊕ Coda

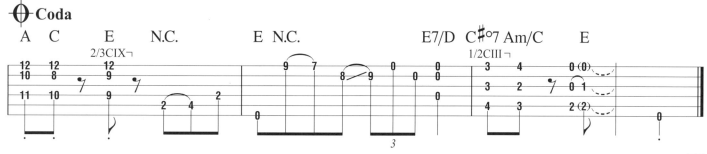

Julia

Words and Music by John Lennon and Paul McCartney

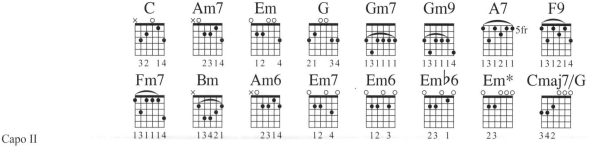

Key of D (Capo Key of C)

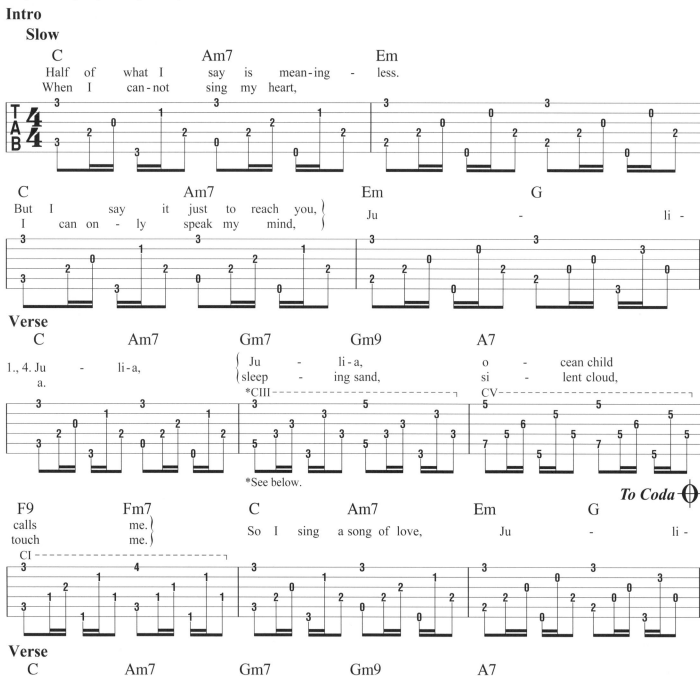

*"C" denotes barre. Fractional prefix indicates which strings are barred (e.g. 1/2 = first 3 strings).
Roman numeral suffix indicates barred fret.

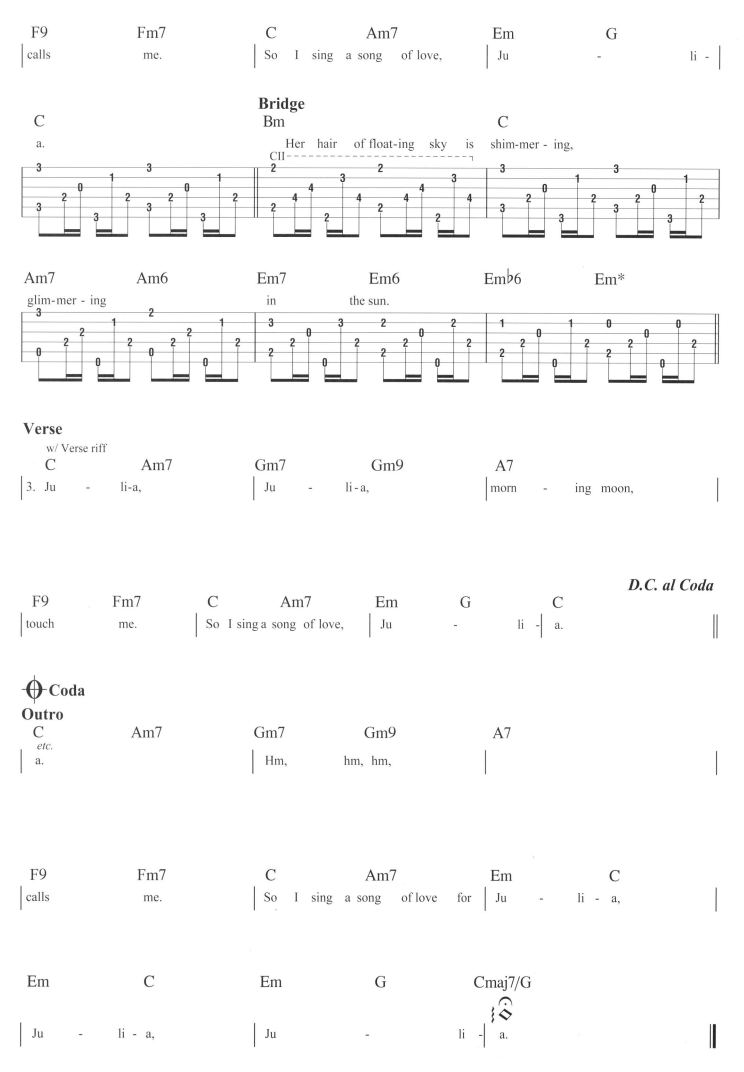

Little Martha

By Duane Allman

Open E tuning:
(low to high) E-B-E-G#-B-E

Key of E

Free time

*Two gtrs. arr. for one.

**CV — — — — — — — —

**See below.

3rd time, To Coda

**"C" denotes barre. Fractional prefix indicates which strings are barred (e.g. 1/2 = first 3 strings).
Roman numeral suffix indicates barred fret.

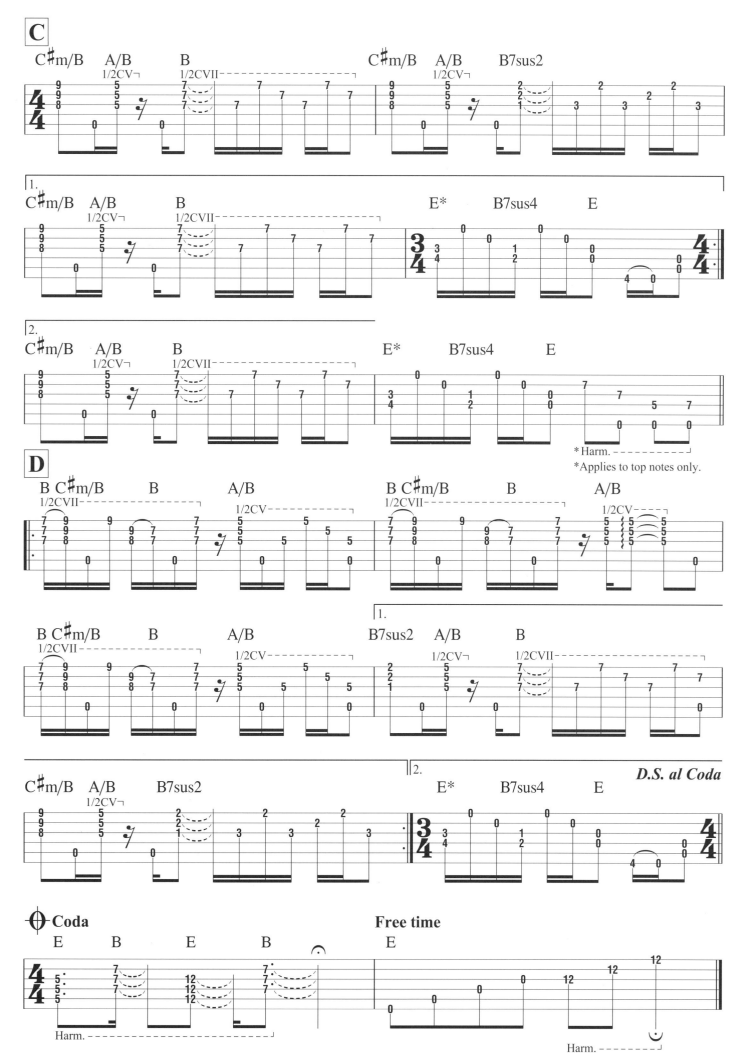

Make Me a Pallet on the Floor

Words and Music by "Mississippi" John Hurt

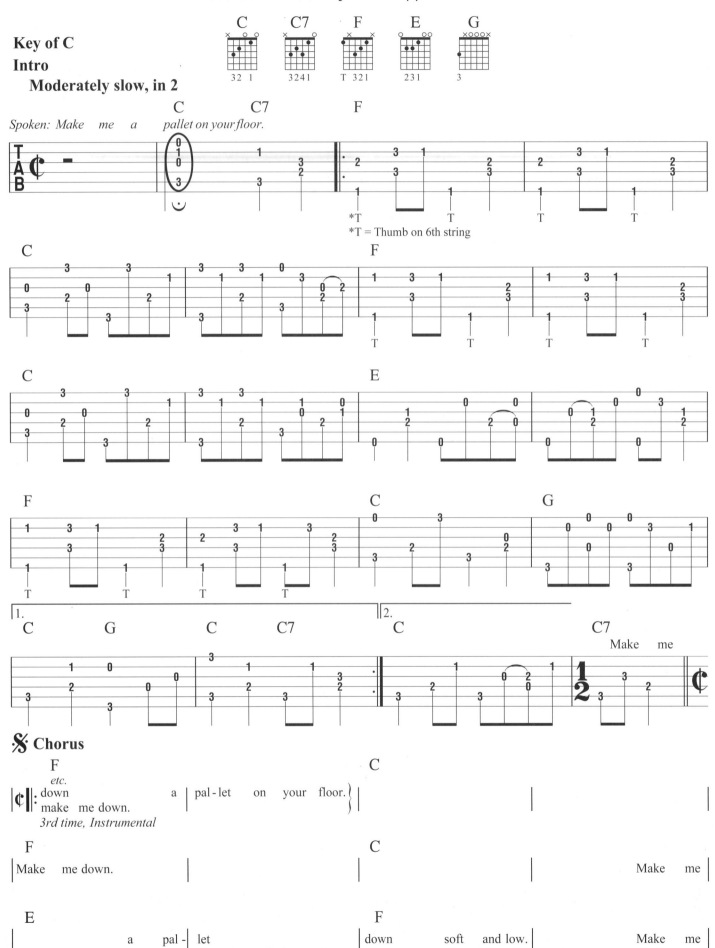

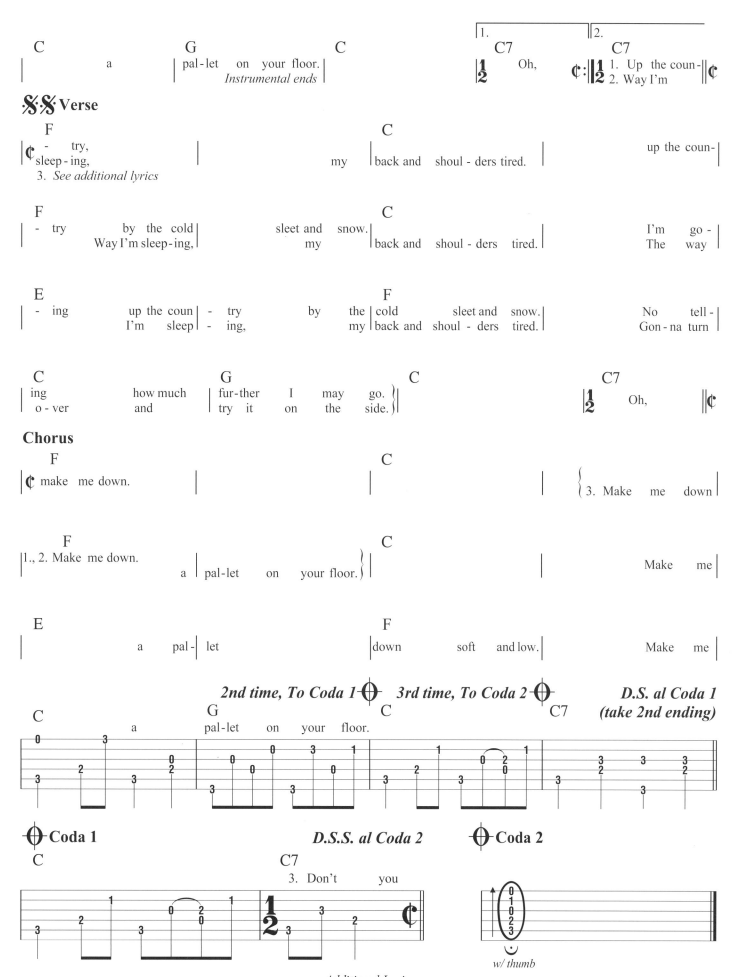

Additional Lyrics

3. Don't you let my good girl catch you here.
   Please don't let my good girl catch you here.
   Oh, she might shoot you, might cut and stab you, too.
   No telling what she might do.

Million Years Ago

Words and Music by Adele Adkins and Gregory Kurstin

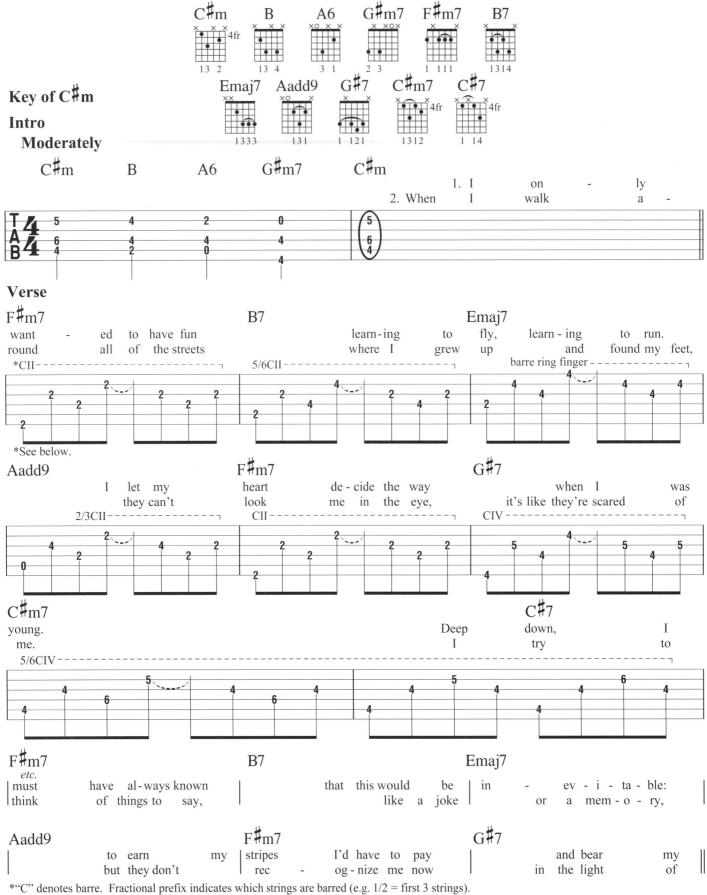

*"C" denotes barre. Fractional prefix indicates which strings are barred (e.g. 1/2 = first 3 strings).
Roman numeral suffix indicates barred fret.

Interlude

C#m7   B   Aadd9   C#m7   B   Aadd9

soul.
day.

C#m7   B   Aadd9   G#7   I   know   I'm

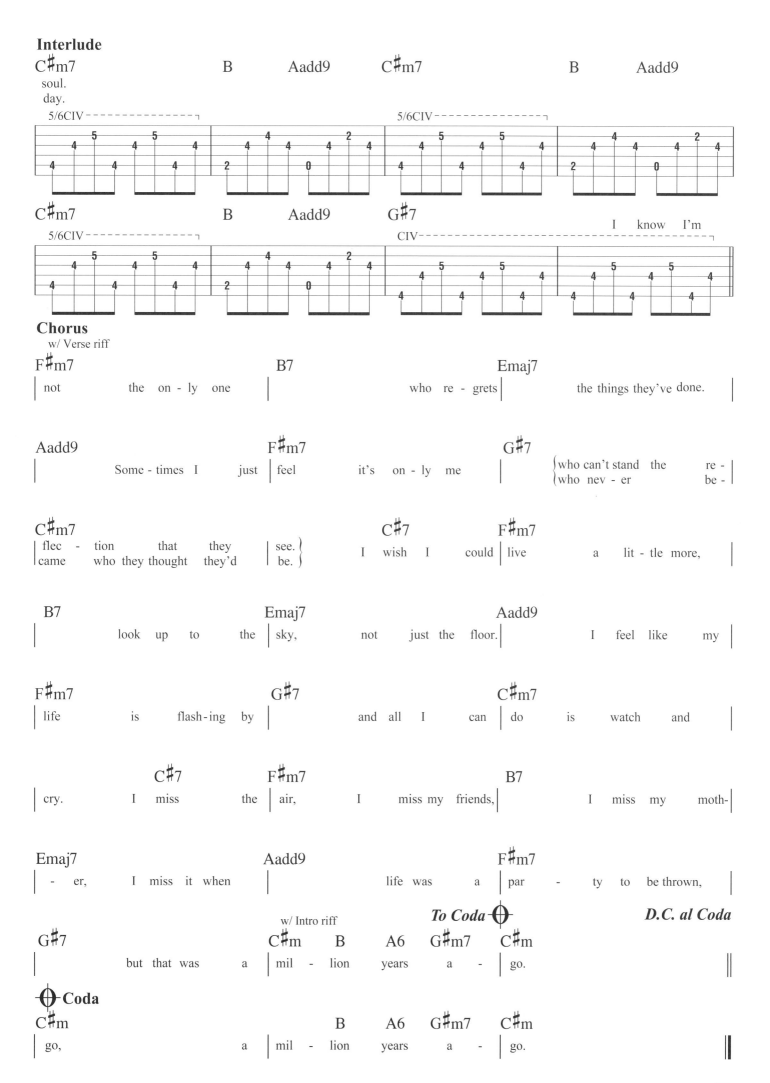

Chorus

w/ Verse riff

F#m7   B7   Emaj7

| not   the   on - ly   one | who   re - grets| the   things   they've   done. |

Aadd9   F#m7   G#7

| Some - times   I   just |feel   it's   on - ly   me | {who can't stand   the   re - |
| | | {who nev - er   be - |

C#m7   C#7   F#m7

| flec - tion   that   they |see.}   I   wish   I   could |live   a   lit - tle more, |
| came   who they thought   they'd |be.} | |

B7   Emaj7   Aadd9

| look   up   to   the |sky,   not   just   the   floor.| I   feel   like   my |

F#m7   G#7   C#m7

| life   is   flash-ing   by | and   all   I   can |do   is   watch   and |

        C#7   F#m7   B7

| cry.   I   miss   the |air,   I   miss   my   friends,| I   miss   my   moth-|

Emaj7   Aadd9   F#m7

| - er,   I   miss   it   when | life   was   a |par - ty   to   be thrown, |

w/ Intro riff   *To Coda* ⊕   *D.C. al Coda*

G#7   C#m   B   A6   G#m7   C#m

| but   that   was   a |mil - lion   years   a - |go.   ‖

⊕ **Coda**

C#m   B   A6   G#m7   C#m

| go,   a |mil - lion   years   a - |go.   ‖

Mona Ray

By Leo Kottke

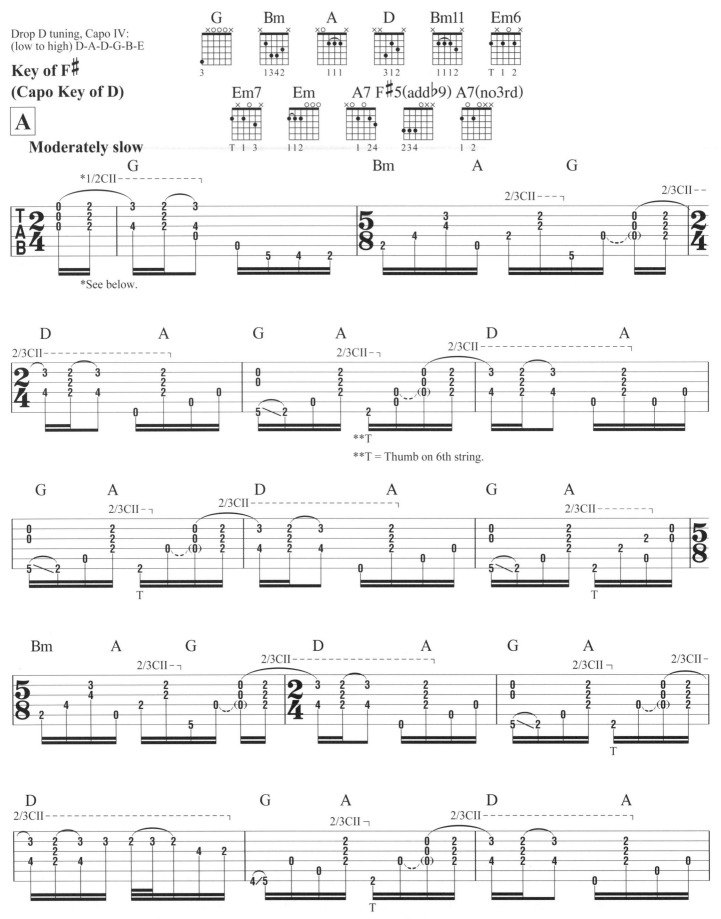

Drop D tuning, Capo IV:
(low to high) D-A-D-G-B-E

Key of F#

(Capo Key of D)

Moderately slow

*See below.

**T = Thumb on 6th string.

*"C" denotes barre. Fractional prefix indicates which strings are barred (e.g. 1/2 = first 3 strings).
  Roman numeral suffix indicates barred fret.

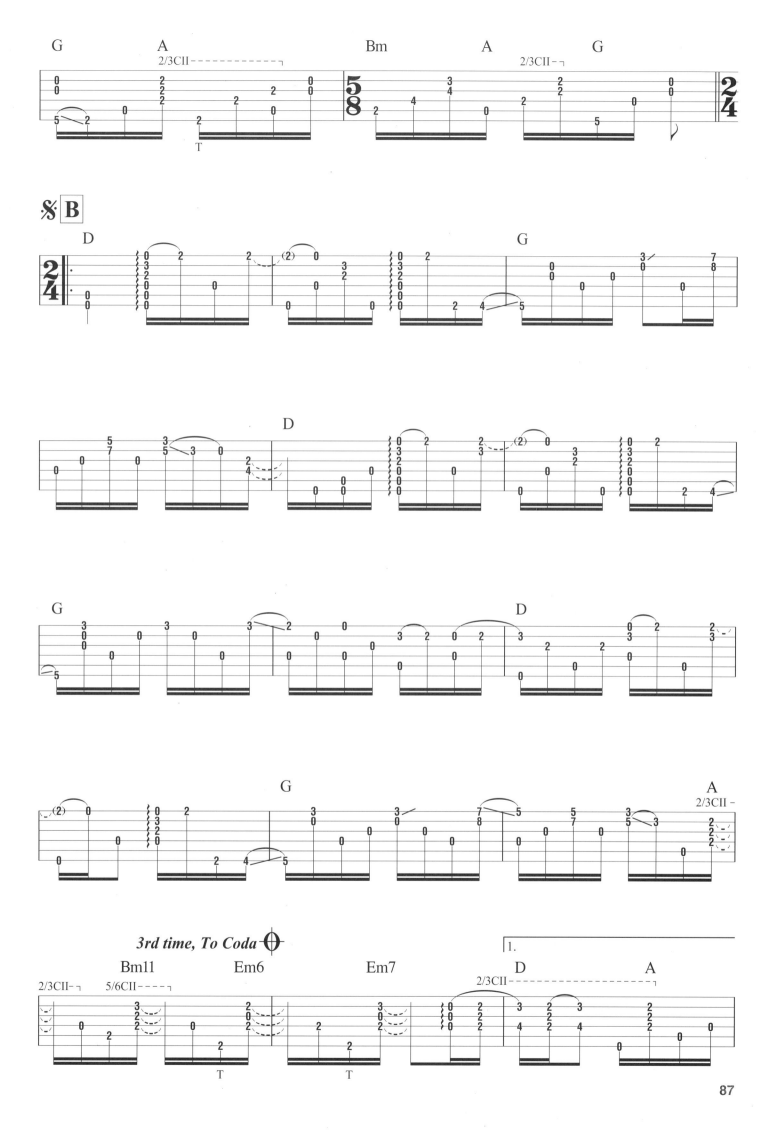

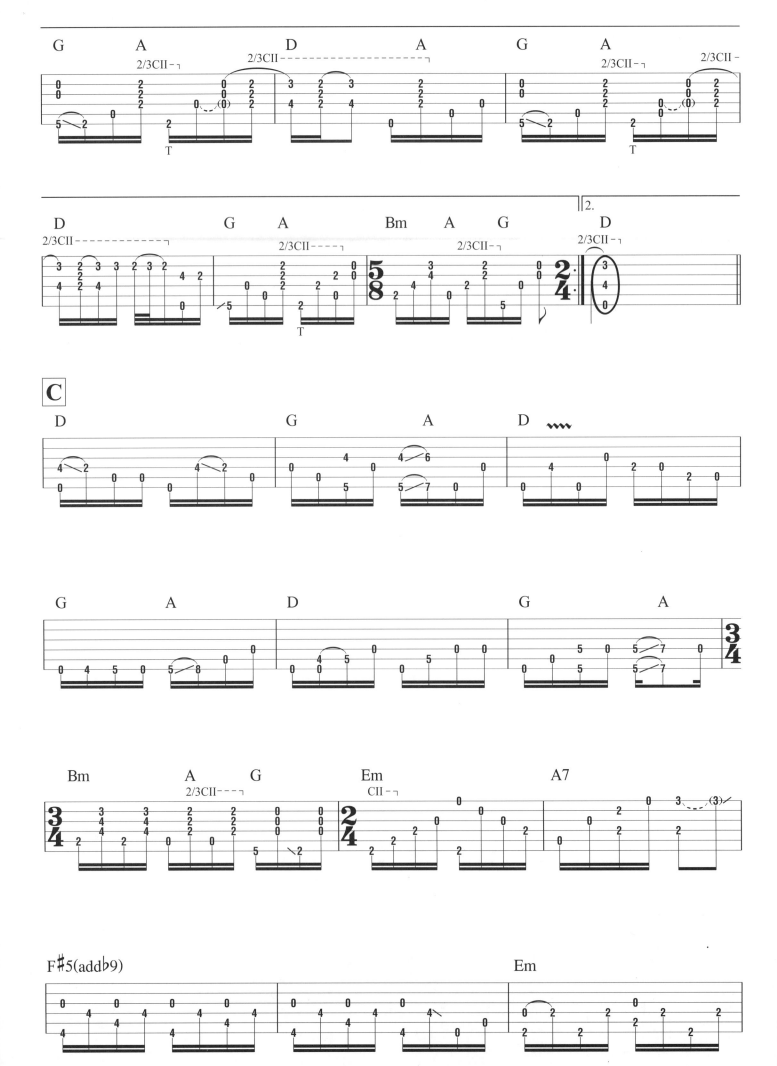

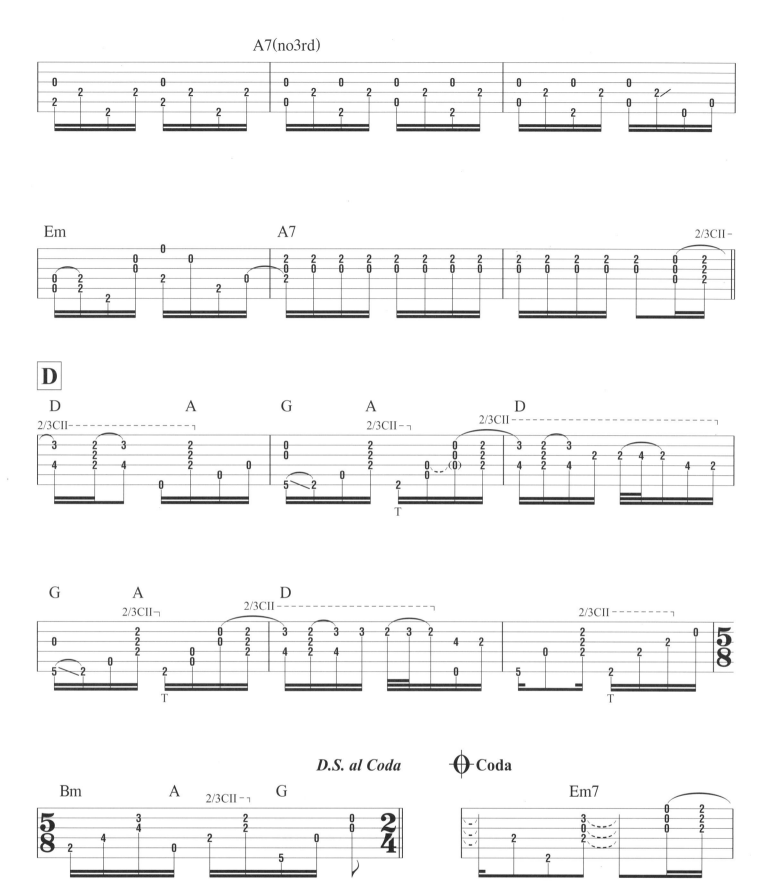

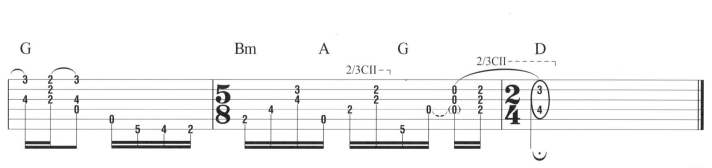

Mood for a Day

Words and Music by Steve Howe

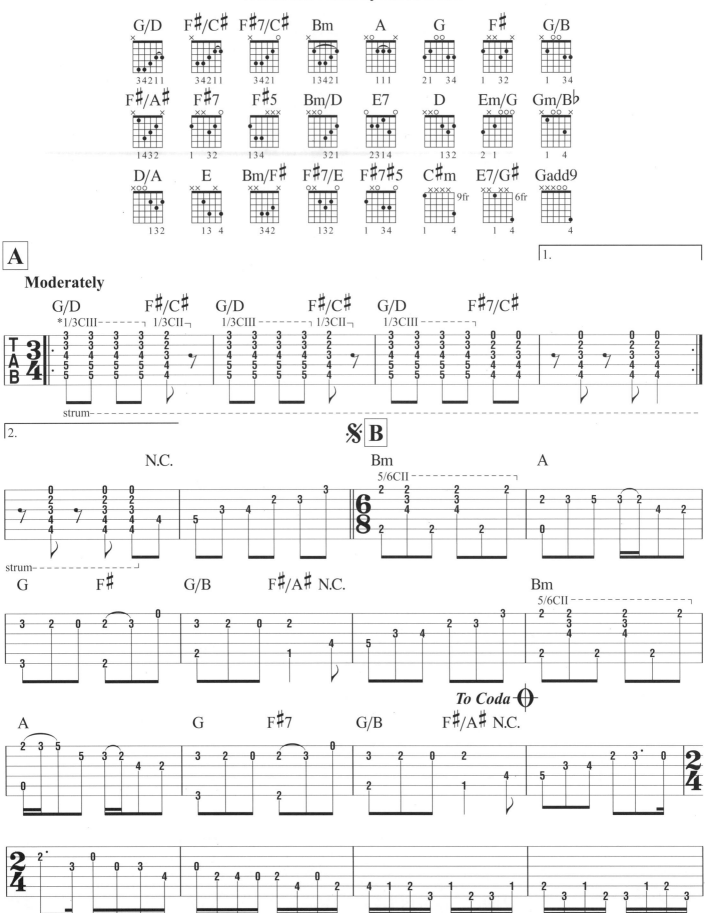

*"C" denotes barre. Fractional prefix indicates which strings are barred (e.g. 1/2 = first 3 strings).
 Roman numeral suffix indicates barred fret.

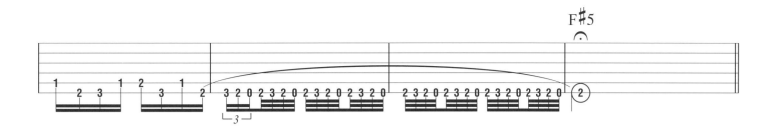

C

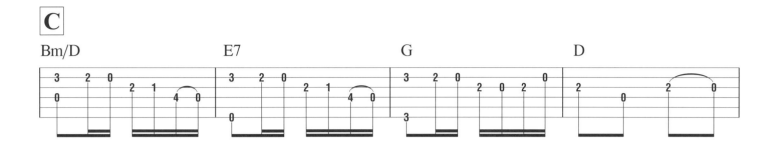

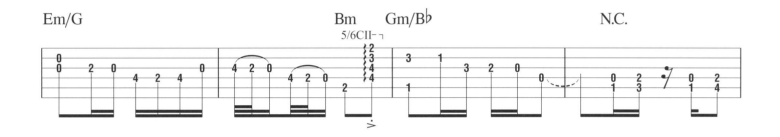

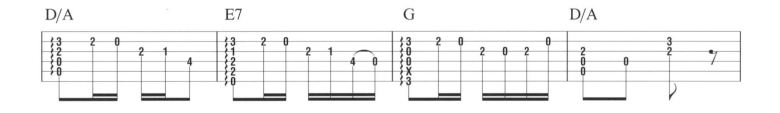

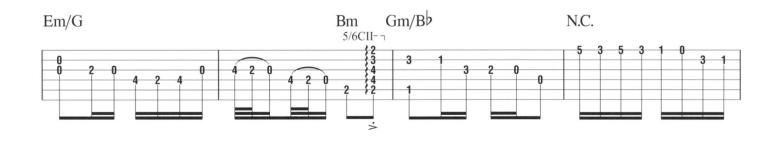

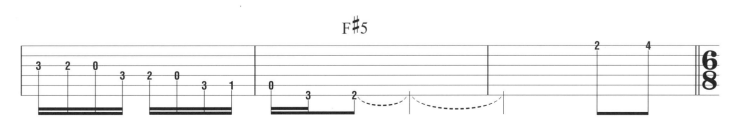

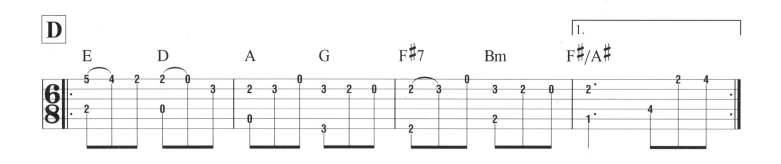

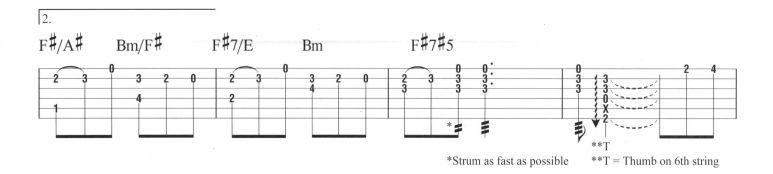

*Strum as fast as possible   **T = Thumb on 6th string

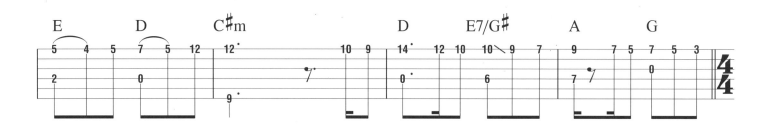

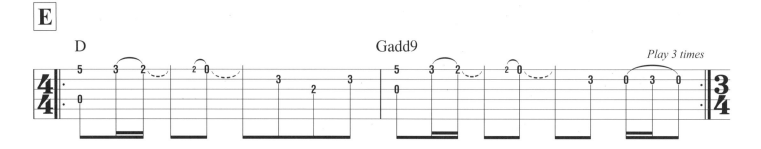

Play 3 times

D.S. al Coda

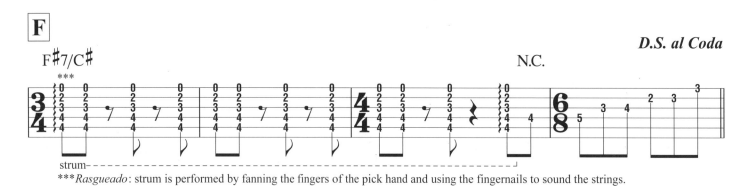

strum- -

***Rasgueado: strum is performed by fanning the fingers of the pick hand and using the fingernails to sound the strings.

Coda

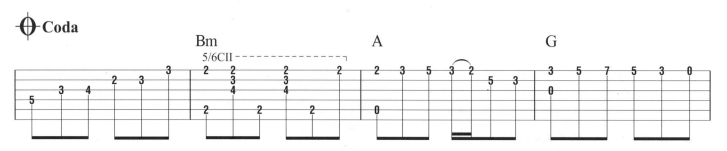

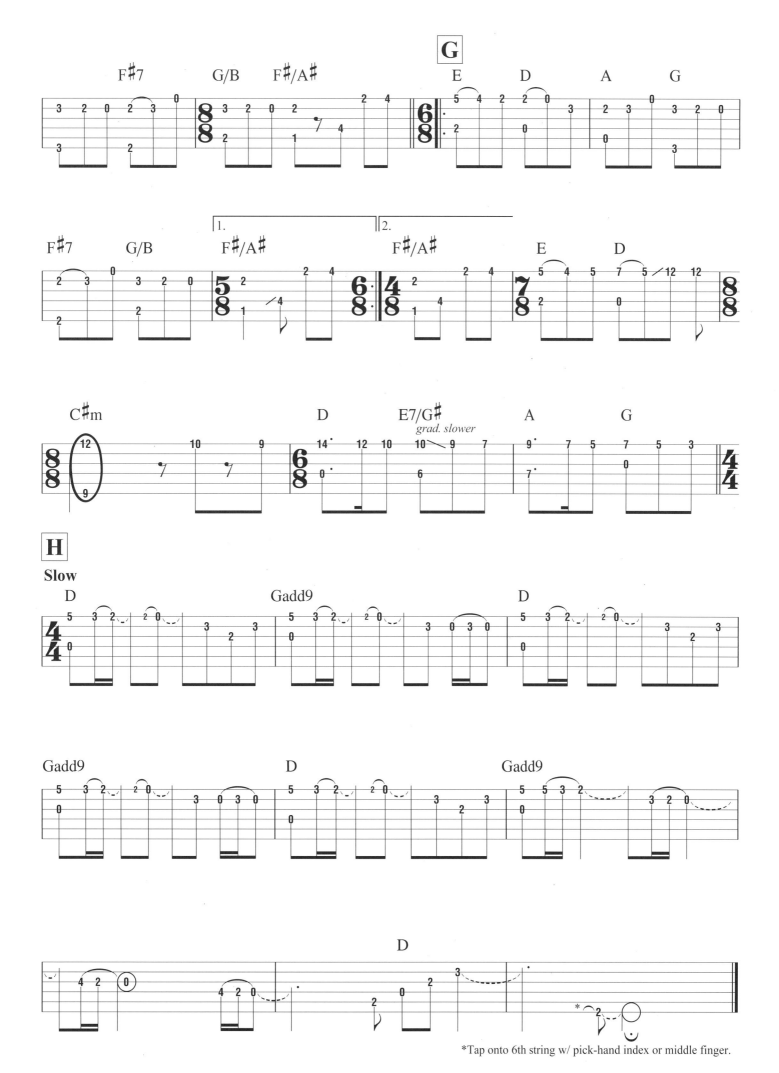

*Tap onto 6th string w/ pick-hand index or middle finger.

Needle of Death

Words and Music by Bert Jansch

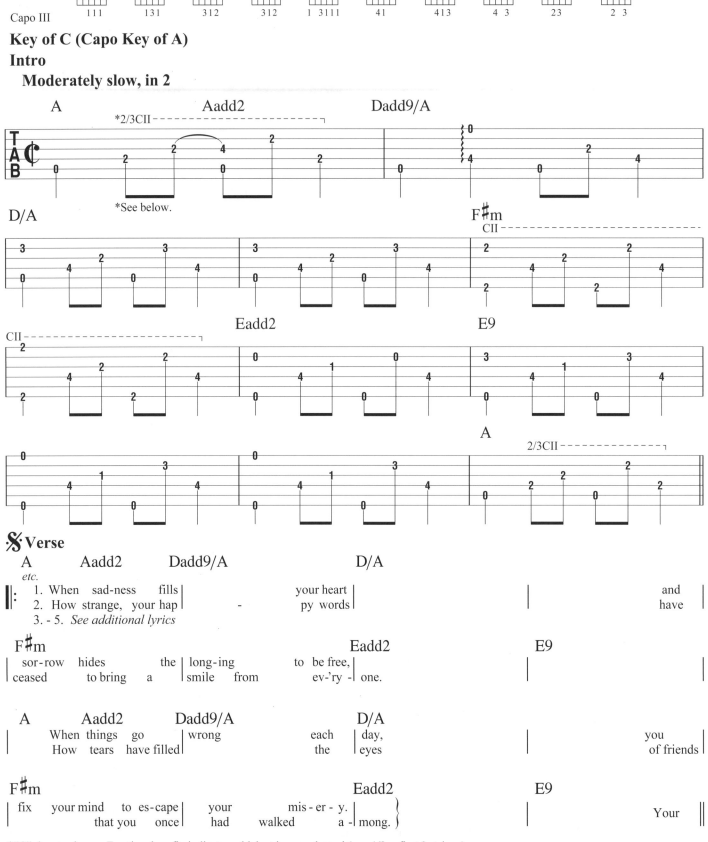

Capo III

Key of C (Capo Key of A)

Intro

Moderately slow, in 2

Verse

A   Aadd2   Dadd9/A   D/A
etc.

‖: 1. When sad-ness fills | your heart | | and |
   2. How strange, your hap | - py words | | have |
   3. - 5. *See additional lyrics*

F#m   Eadd2   E9
| sor-row hides the | long-ing to be free, | | |
| ceased to bring a | smile from ev'ry - | one. | |

A   Aadd2   Dadd9/A   D/A
| When things go | wrong each | day, | | you |
| How tears have filled | the | eyes | | of friends |

F#m   Eadd2   E9
| fix your mind to es-cape | your mis-er - y. ⎫| | Your ‖
| that you once had walked a - | mong. ⎭| |

*"C" denotes barre. Fractional prefix indicates which strings are barred (e.g. 1/2 = first 3 strings).
Roman numeral suffix indicates barred fret.

Chorus

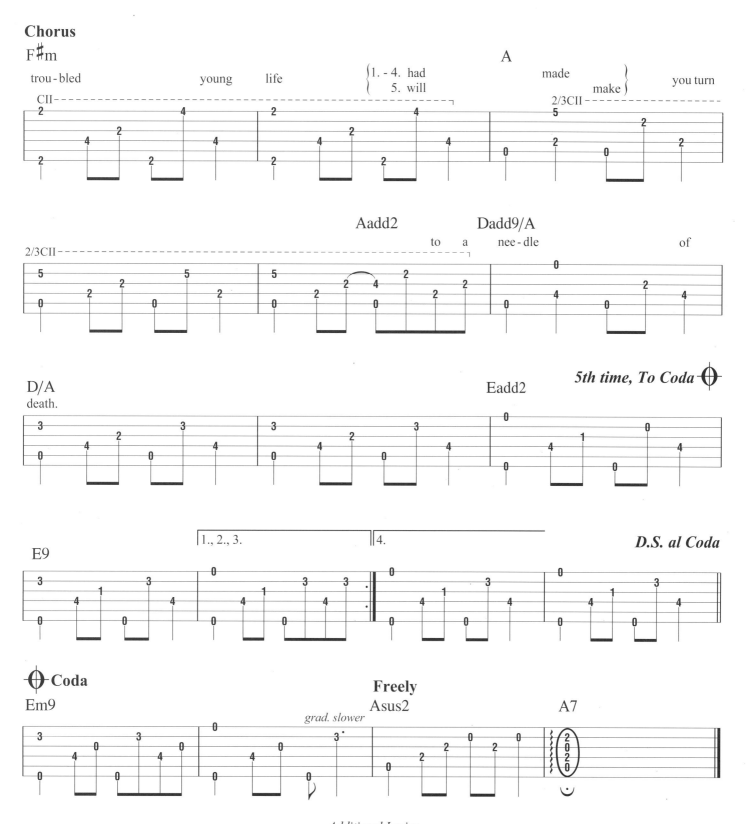

Additional Lyrics

3. One grain of pure white snow
   Dissolved in blood spread quickly to your brain.
   In peace, your mind withdraws,
   Your death so near, your soul can feel no pain.

4. Your mother stands a cryin'
   While to the earth your body's slowly cast.
   Your father stands in silence,
   Caressing ev'ry young dream of the past.

5. Through ages, man's desires
   To free his mind, to release his very soul
   Has proved to all who live
   That death itself is freedom forevermore.

Never Going Back Again

Words and Music by Lindsey Buckingham

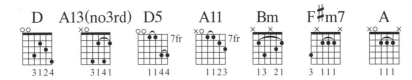

Drop D tuning, Capo IV:
(low to high) D-A-D-G-B-E

Key of F# (Capo Key of D)

Intro

Moderately slow

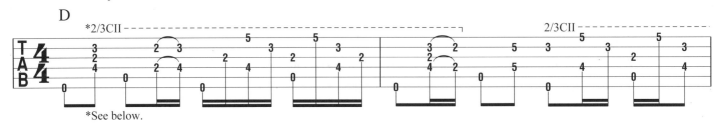

*See below.

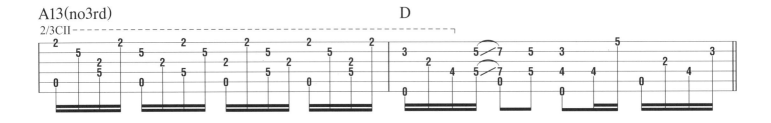

𝄋 Verse

w/ Intro pattern

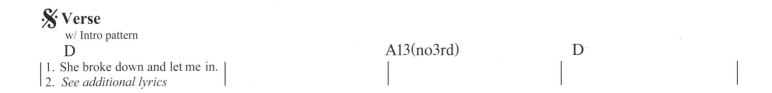

| D | A13(no3rd) | D |

1. She broke down and let me in.
2. *See additional lyrics*

| | A13(no3rd) | D |

Made me see where I've been.

Chorus

| D5 | A11 | D5 | A11 | D5 |

Been down one time, been down two

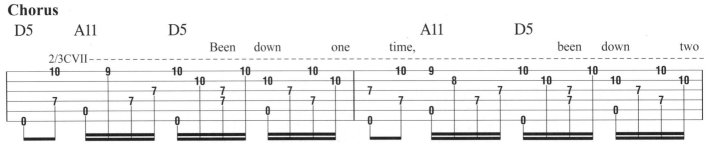

*"C" denotes barre. Fractional prefix indicates which strings are barred (e.g. 1/2 = first 3 strings).
Roman numeral suffix indicates barred fret.

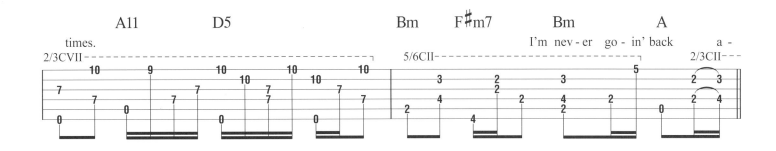

Interlude

To Coda ⊕

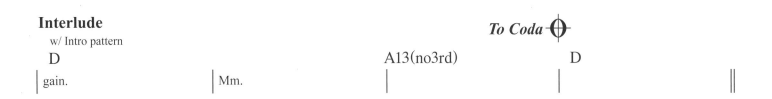

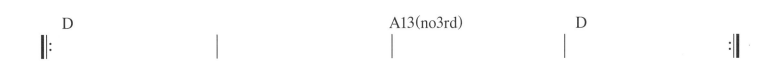

⊕ **Coda**

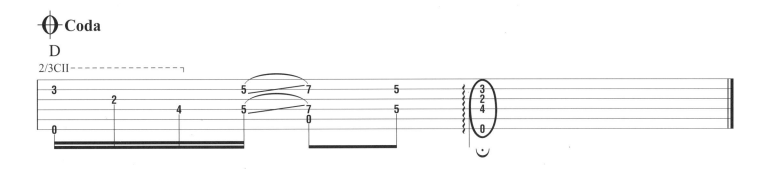

Additional Lyrics

2. You don't know what it means to win.
   Come down and see me again.

Nine Pound Hammer

Words and Music by Merle Travis

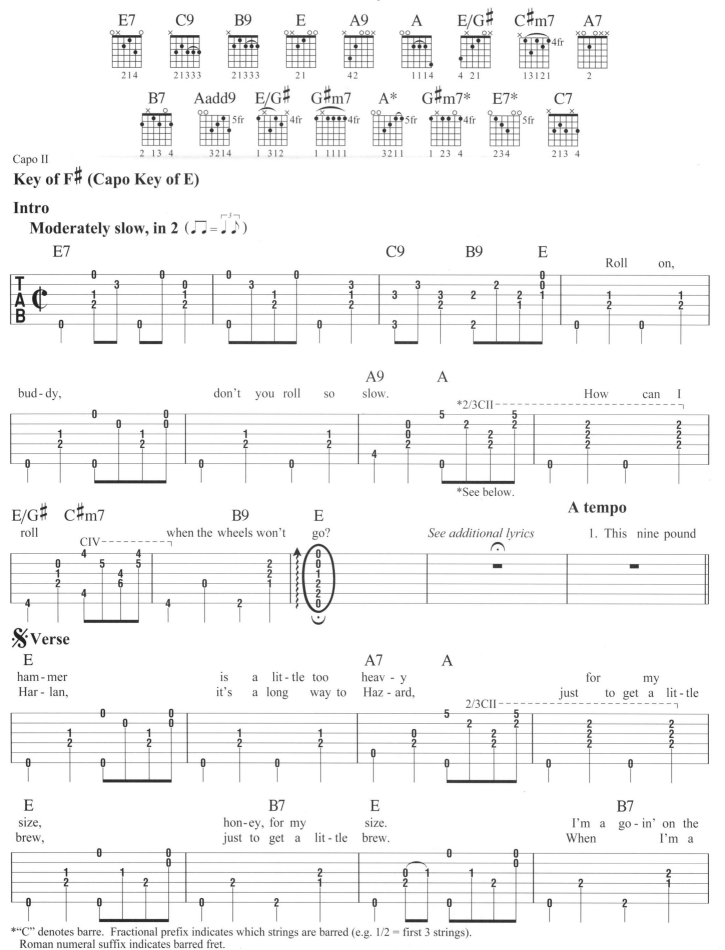

Capo II

Key of F♯ (Capo Key of E)

Intro

Moderately slow, in 2

*"C" denotes barre. Fractional prefix indicates which strings are barred (e.g. 1/2 = first 3 strings).
Roman numeral suffix indicates barred fret.

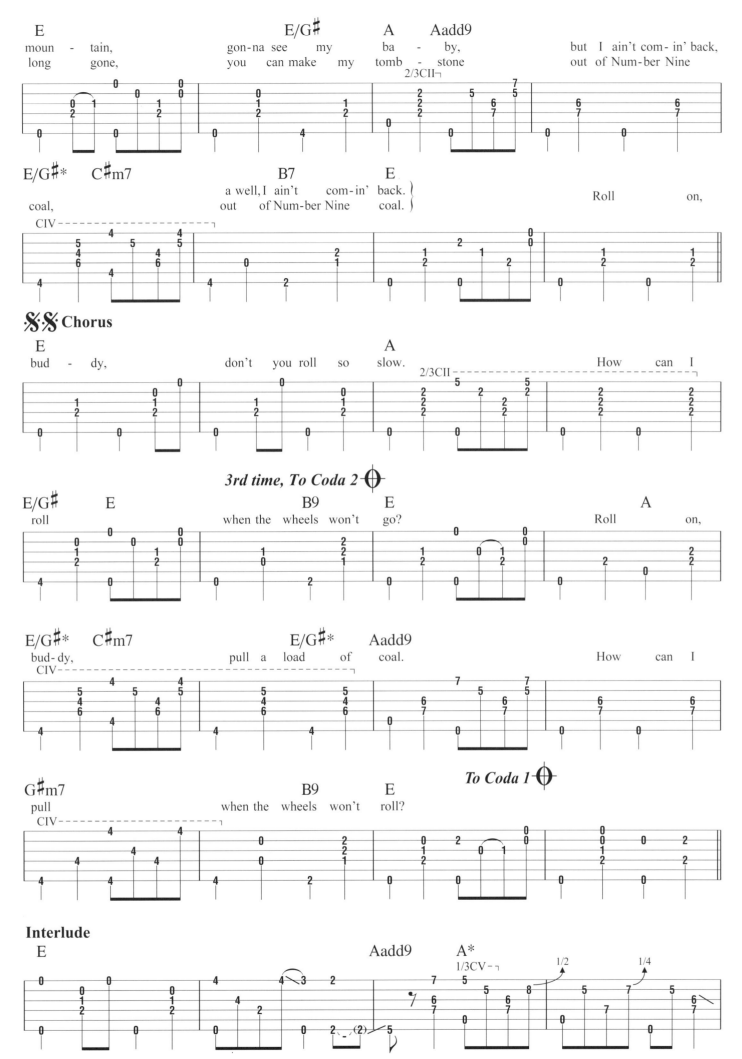

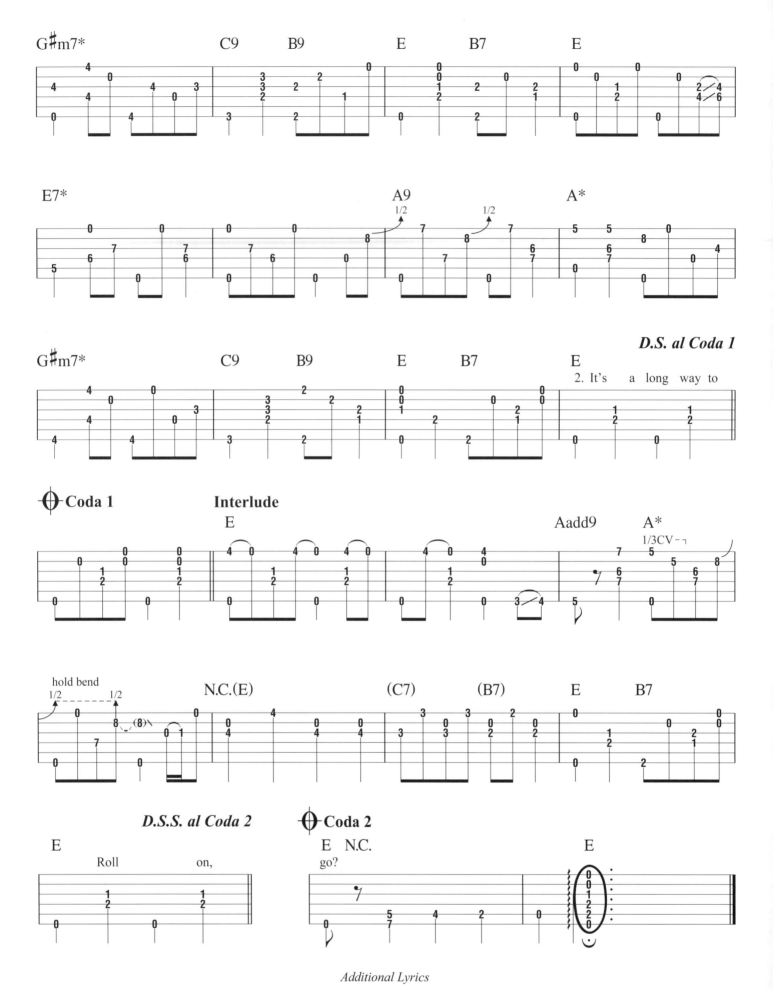

Additional Lyrics

*Intro Up in East Kentucky around Harlan and Perry County the coal miner sings a little song called "The Nine Pound Hammer."
Now just picture yourself a drivin' four-inch spikes in hard, black oak track ties about five miles back under the mountain,
where the top's so low in the mines that you can't straighten up to rest your back just for a minute, and lots of times the air
gets so foul back there that you just can't get a good, deep breath.*

Sailing to Philadelphia

Words and Music by Mark Knopfler

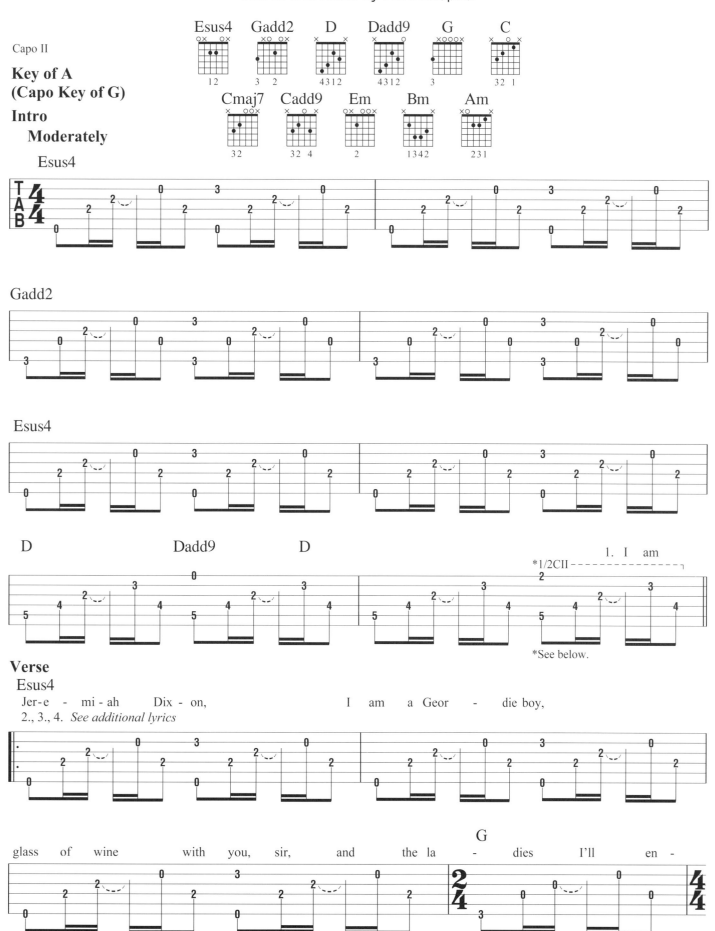

*"C" denotes barre. Fractional prefix indicates which strings are barred (e.g. 1/2 = first 3 strings).
Roman numeral suffix indicates barred fret.

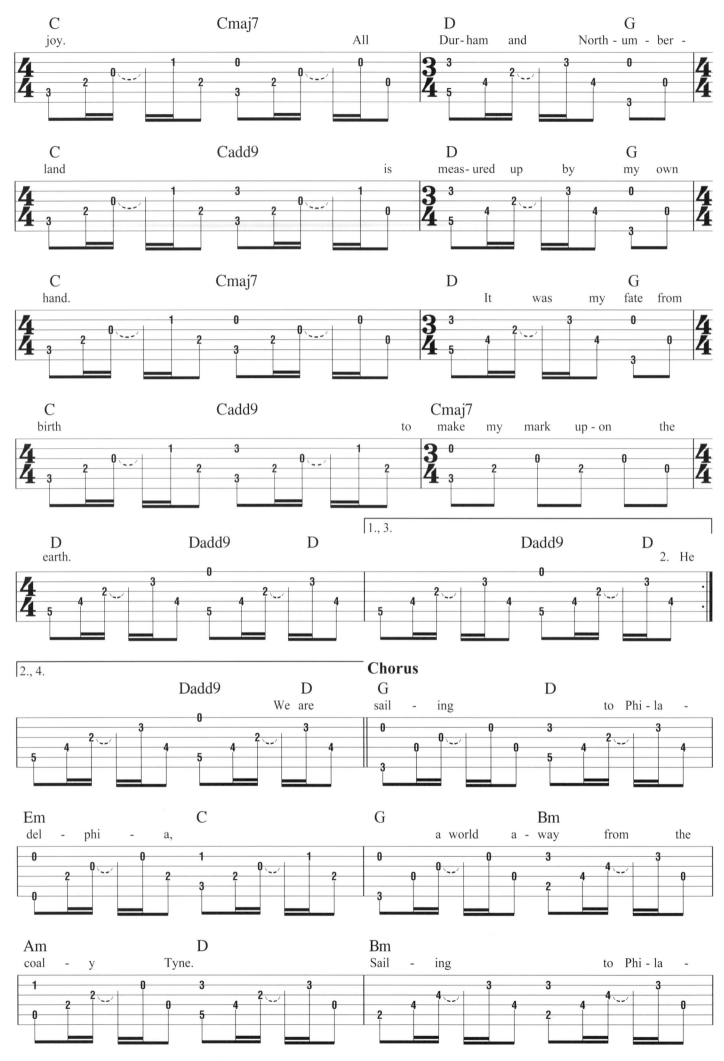

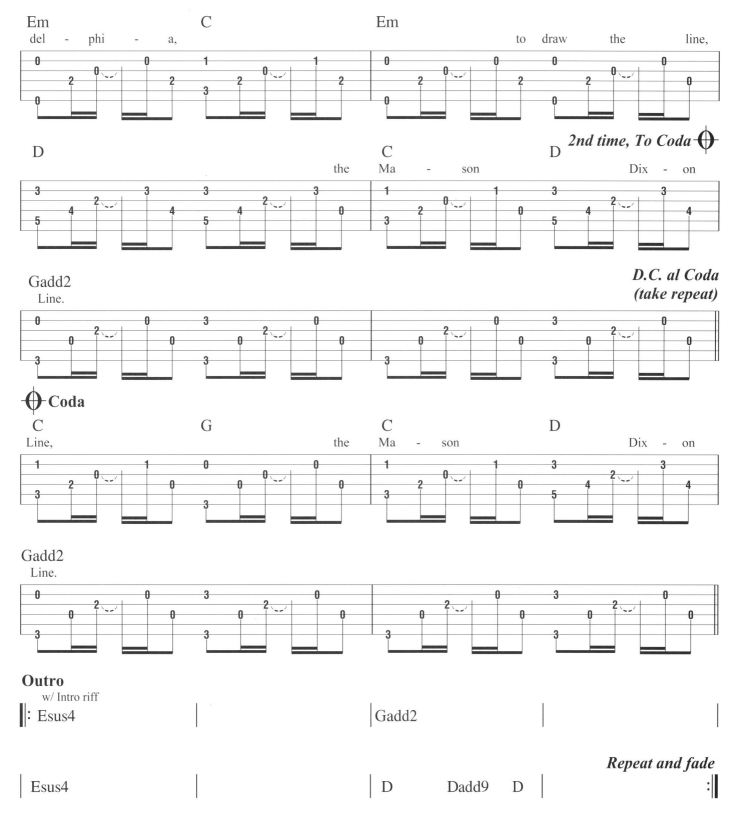

Outro
w/ Intro riff

‖: Esus4 | | Gadd2 | |

Repeat and fade

Esus4 | | D   Dadd9   D | :‖

Additional Lyrics

2. He calls me Charlie Mason, a stargazer am I,
   It seems that I was born to chart the evening sky.
   They'd cut me out for baking bread, but I had other dreams instead.
   This baker's boy from the west country would join the Royal Society.

3. Now you're a good surveyor, Dixon, but I swear you'll make me mad.
   The West will kill us both, you gullible Geordie lad.
   You talk of liberty. How can America be free?
   A Geordie and a baker's boy in the forests of the Iroquois.

4. Now hold your head up, Mason, see America lies there.
   The morning tide has raised the capes of Delaware.
   Come up and feel the sun, a new morning is begun.
   Another day will make it clear why your stars should guide us here.

Puff the Magic Dragon

Words and Music by Lenny Lipton and Peter Yarrow

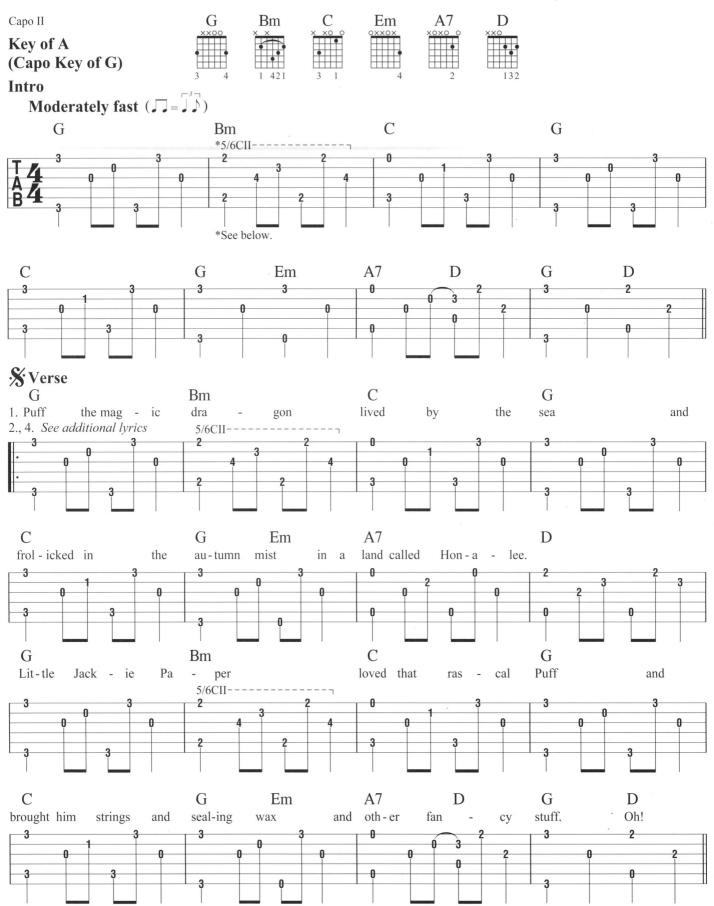

*"C" denotes barre. Fractional prefix indicates which strings are barred (e.g. 1/2 = first 3 strings).
   Roman numeral suffix indicates barred fret.

Chorus
w/ Verse pattern

G	Bm	C	G
Puff the mag - ic	dra - gon	lived by the	sea and

C	G Em A7	D	
frol-icked in the	au-tumn mist in a	land called Hon-a - lee.	

G	Bm	C	G
Puff the mag - ic	dra - gon	lived by the	sea and

3rd time, To Coda ⊕ |1. |2.

C	G Em A7 D	G D	G D
frol-icked in the	au-tumn mist in a	land called Hon-a - lee.	:‖ 3. A ‖

Verse
w/ Verse pattern

G	Bm	C	G
drag - on lives for -	ev - er, but	not so lit-tle boys.	

C	G Em A7	D	
Paint - ed wings and	gi-ant rings make	way for oth-er toys.	

G	Bm	C	G
One gray night it hap -	pened, Jack-ie Pa -	per came no	more, and

D.S. al Coda

C	G Em A7 D	G D	
Puff that might-y drag -	on, he	ceased his fear - less roar.	4. His ‖

⊕ Coda

A7	D	G
land called Hon - a -	lee.	

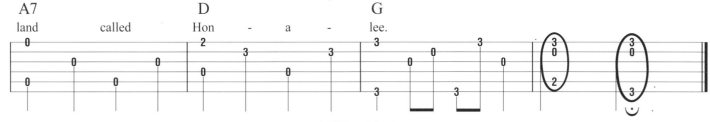

Additional Lyrics

2. Together they would travel on a boat with billowed sail.
    Jackie kept a lookout perched on Puff's gigantic tail.
    Noble kings and princes would bow when e'er they came.
    Pirate ships would low'r their flags when Puff roared out his name. Oh!

4. His head was bent in sorrow, green scales fell like rain.
    Puff no longer went to play along the Cherry Lane.
    Without his lifelong friend, Puff could not be brave.
    So Puff, that mighty dragon sadly slipped into his cave. Oh!

Road Trippin'

Words and Music by Anthony Kiedis, Flea, John Frusciante and Chad Smith

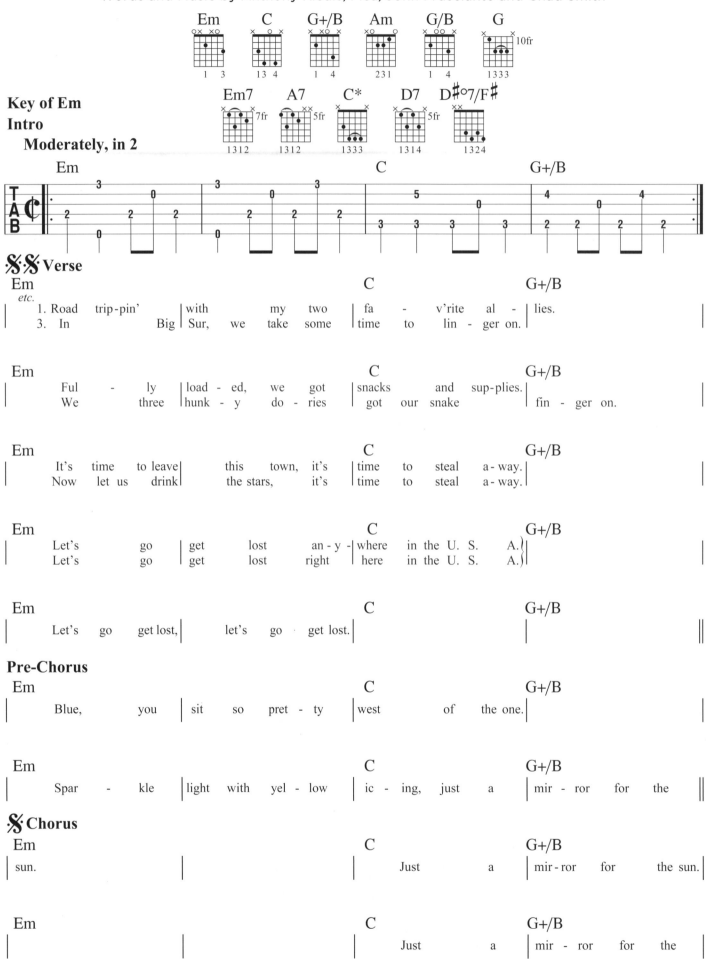

106

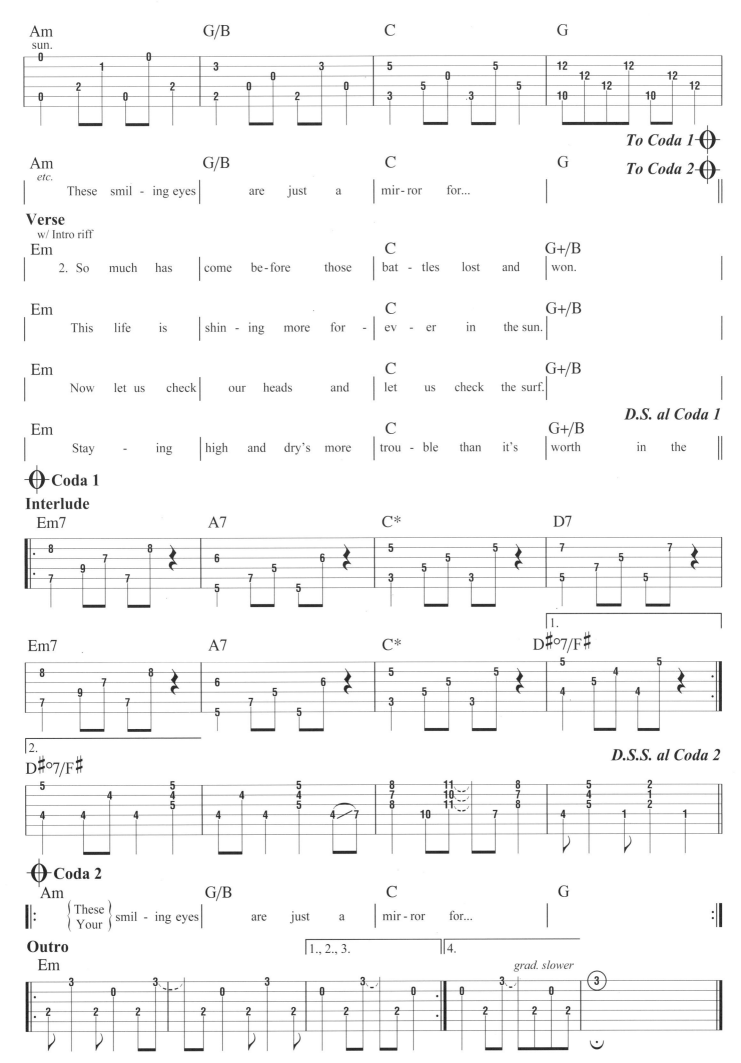

107

Shape of My Heart

Music by Sting and Dominic Miller
Lyrics by Sting

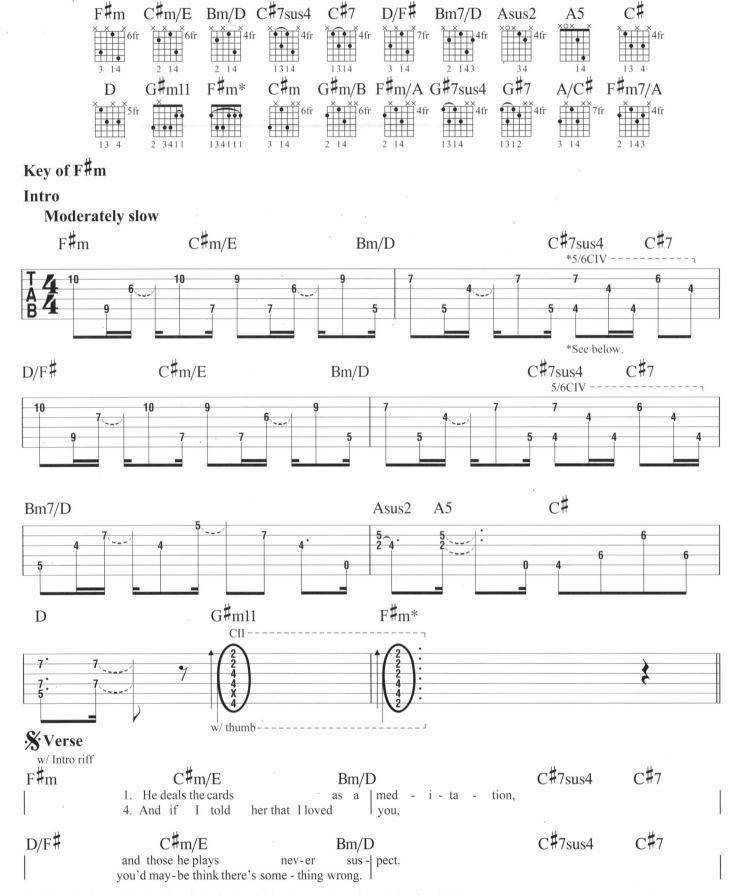

Key of F♯m

Intro

Moderately slow

*"C" denotes barre. Fractional prefix indicates which strings are barred (e.g. 1/2 = first 3 strings). Roman numeral suffix indicates barred fret.

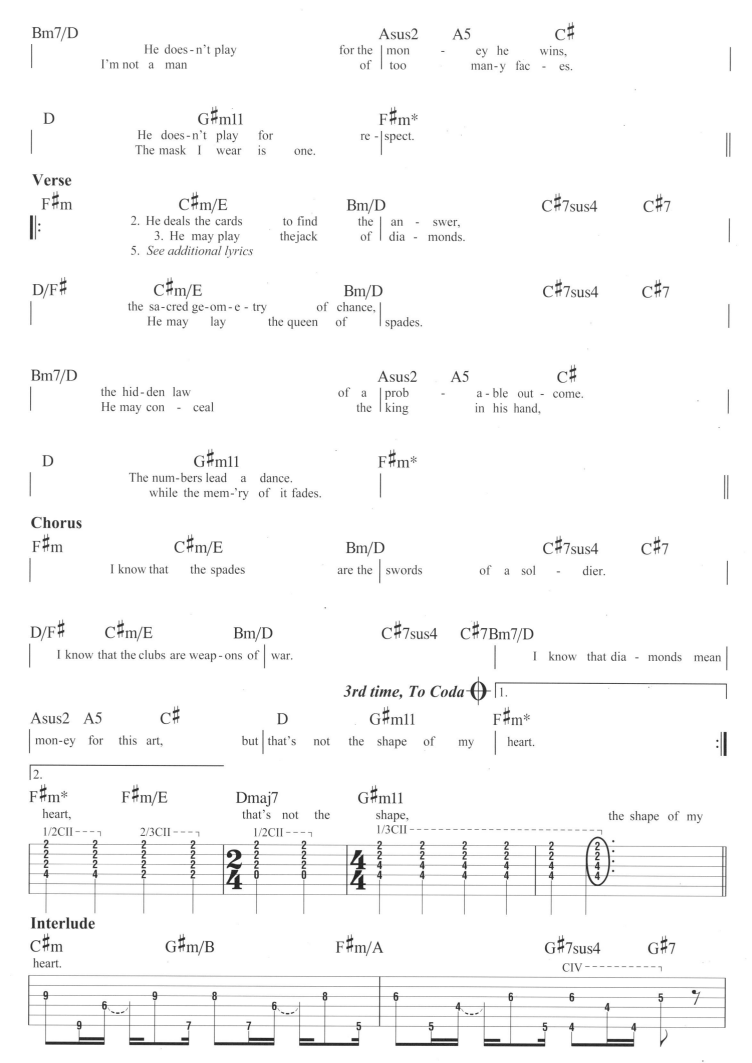

Bm7/D
He does-n't play   for the | mon - ey he   wins,
I'm not a man   of | too   man-y fac - es.

Asus2   A5   C♯

D   G♯m11   F♯m*
He does-n't play for   re - | spect.
The mask I wear is   one.

Verse

F♯m   C♯m/E   Bm/D   C♯7sus4   C♯7
2. He deals the cards   to find   the | an - swer,
3. He may play   thejack   of | dia - monds.
5. *See additional lyrics*

D/F♯   C♯m/E   Bm/D   C♯7sus4   C♯7
the sa-cred ge-om-e-try   of | chance,
He may   lay   the queen of | spades.

Bm7/D   Asus2   A5   C♯
the hid-den law   of a | prob - a-ble out-come.
He may con - ceal   the | king   in his hand,

D   G♯m11   F♯m*
The num-bers lead a   dance.
while the mem-'ry of it fades.

Chorus

F♯m   C♯m/E   Bm/D   C♯7sus4   C♯7
I know that   the spades   are the | swords   of a sol - dier.

D/F♯   C♯m/E   Bm/D   C♯7sus4   C♯7 Bm7/D
I know that the clubs are weap-ons of | war.   I know that dia - monds mean

3rd time, To Coda ⊕ ⌐1.

Asus2 A5   C♯   D   G♯m11   F♯m*
mon-ey for   this art,   but | that's not the shape of my | heart.

⌐2.

F♯m*   F♯m/E   Dmaj7   G♯m11
heart,   that's not the   shape,   the shape of my

Interlude

C♯m   G♯m/B   F♯m/A   G♯7sus4   G♯7
heart.

109

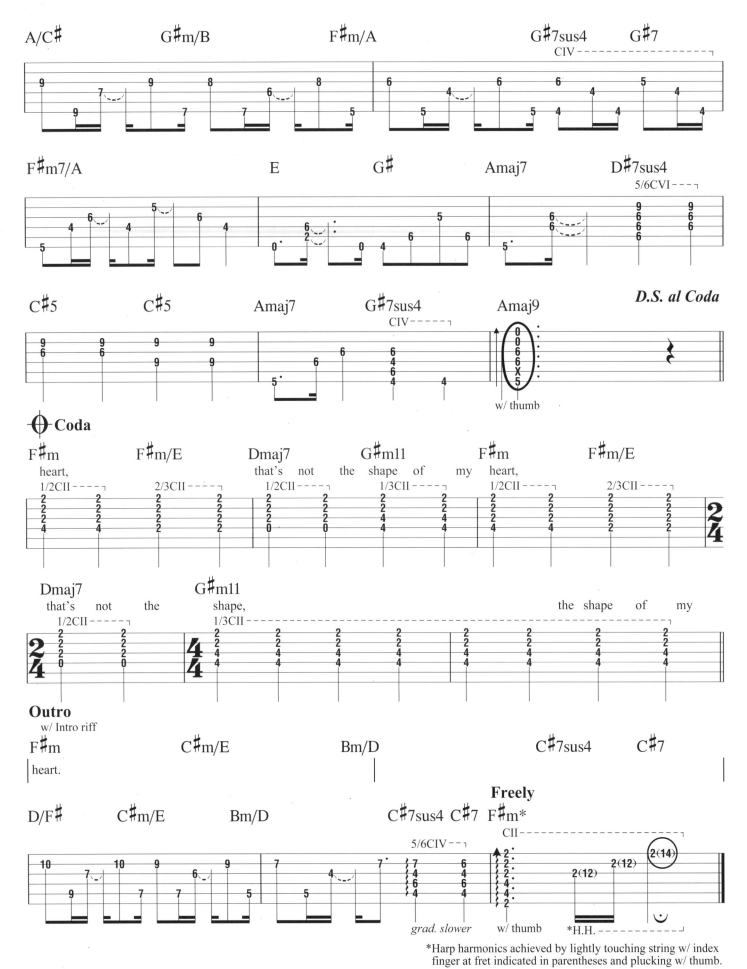

*Harp harmonics achieved by lightly touching string w/ index
finger at fret indicated in parentheses and plucking w/ thumb.

Additional Lyrics

5. Well, those who speak know nothin'
    And find out to their cost,
    Like those who curse their luck in too many places,
    And those who fear are lost.

Stop This Train

Words and Music by John Mayer and Pino Palladino

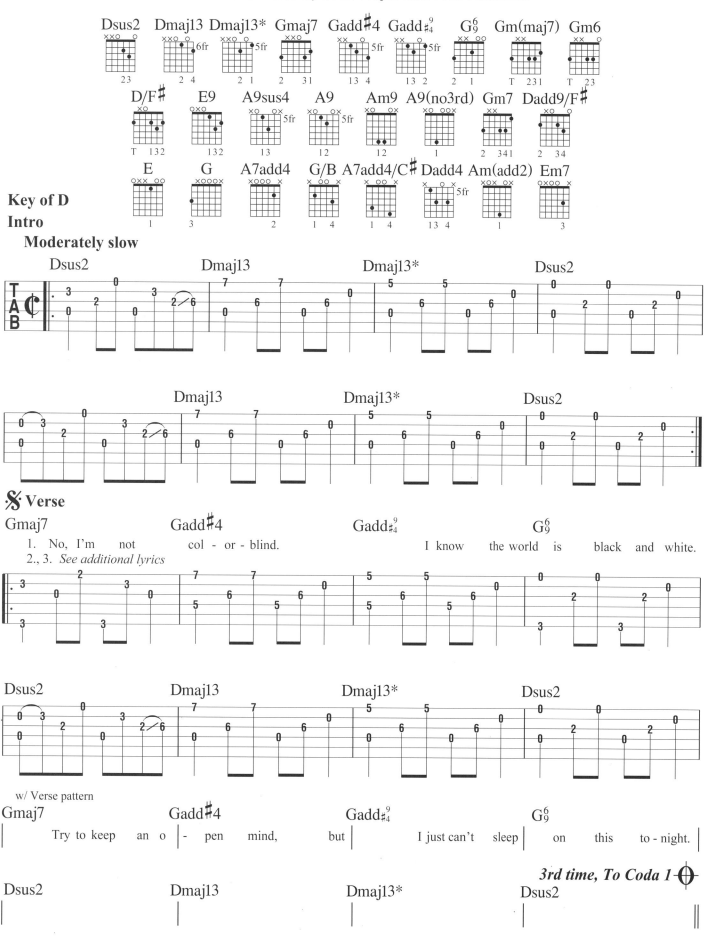

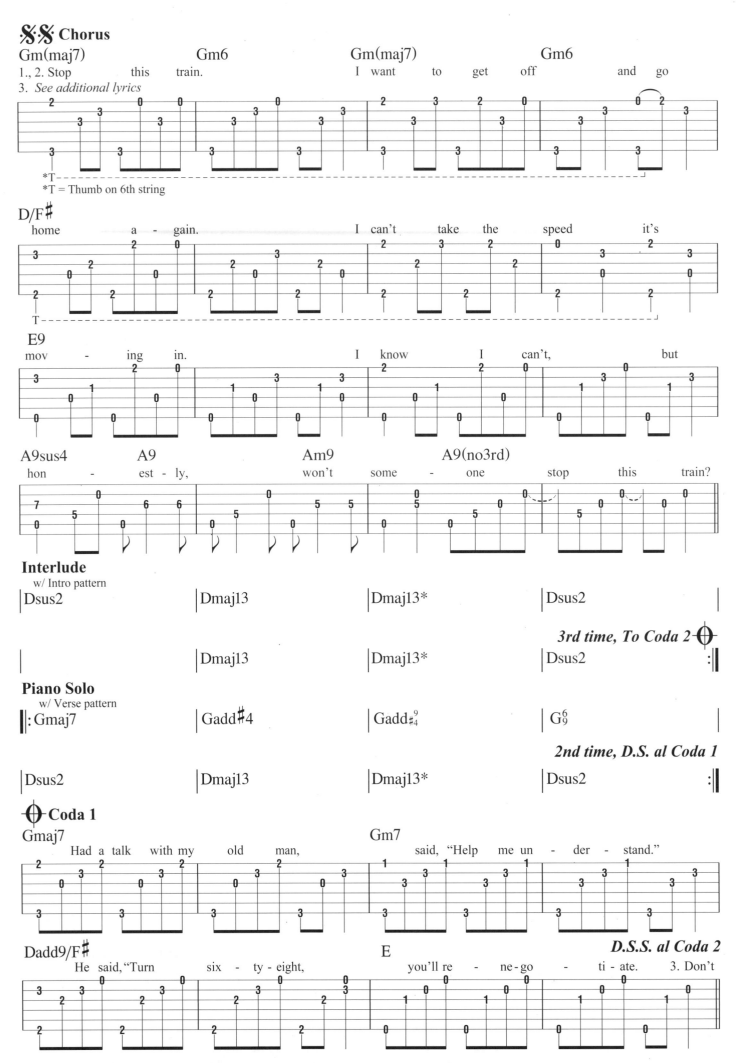

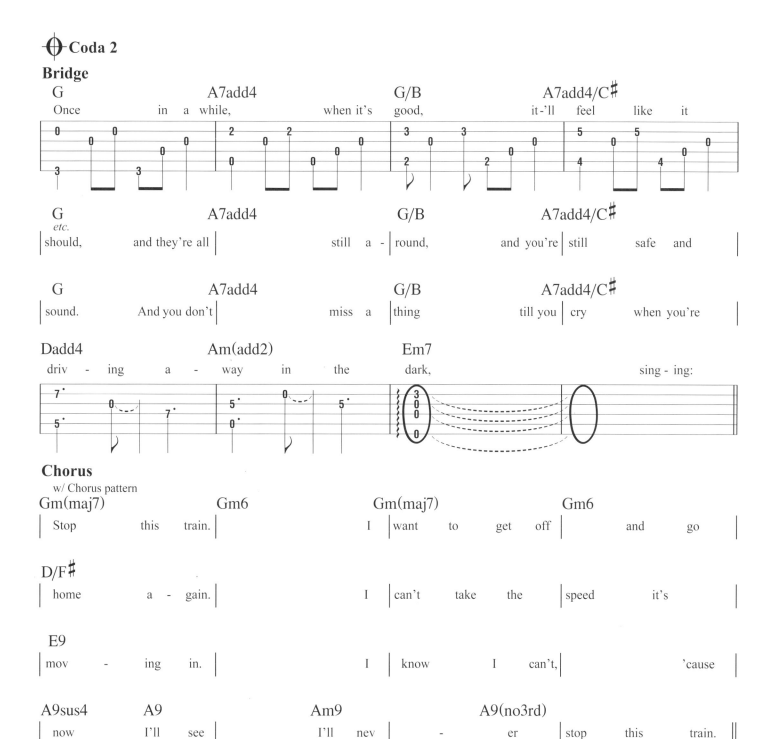

Outro
w/ Intro pattern

Repeat and fade

||: Dsus2 | Dmaj13 | Dmaj13* | Dsus2 :||

Additional Lyrics

2. Don't know how else to say it,
   Don't wanna see my parents go.
   One generation's length away
   From fightin' life out on my own.

3. So scared of gettin' older,
   I'm only good at bein' young.
   So I play the numbers game
   To find a way to say that life has just begun.
   Had a talk with my old man,
   Said, "Help me understand."
   He said, "Turn sixty-eight,
   You'll renegotiate.

Chorus 3 Don't stop this train.
   Don't for a minute change the place you're in.
   And don't think I couldn't ever understand,
   I tried my hand, John, honestly,
   We'll never stop this train."

Tears in Heaven

Words and Music by Eric Clapton and Will Jennings

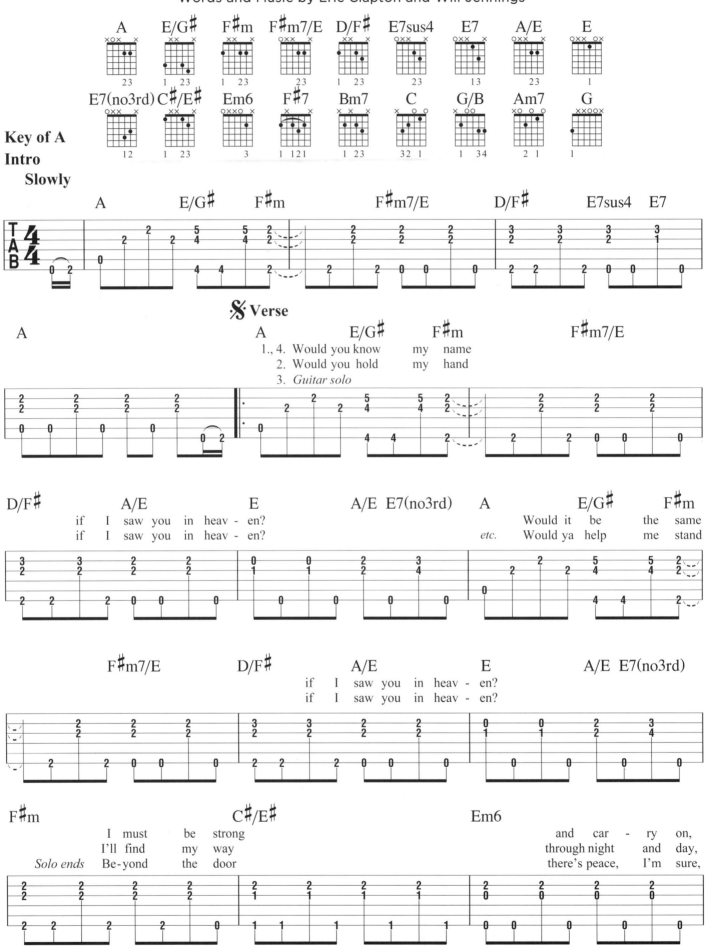

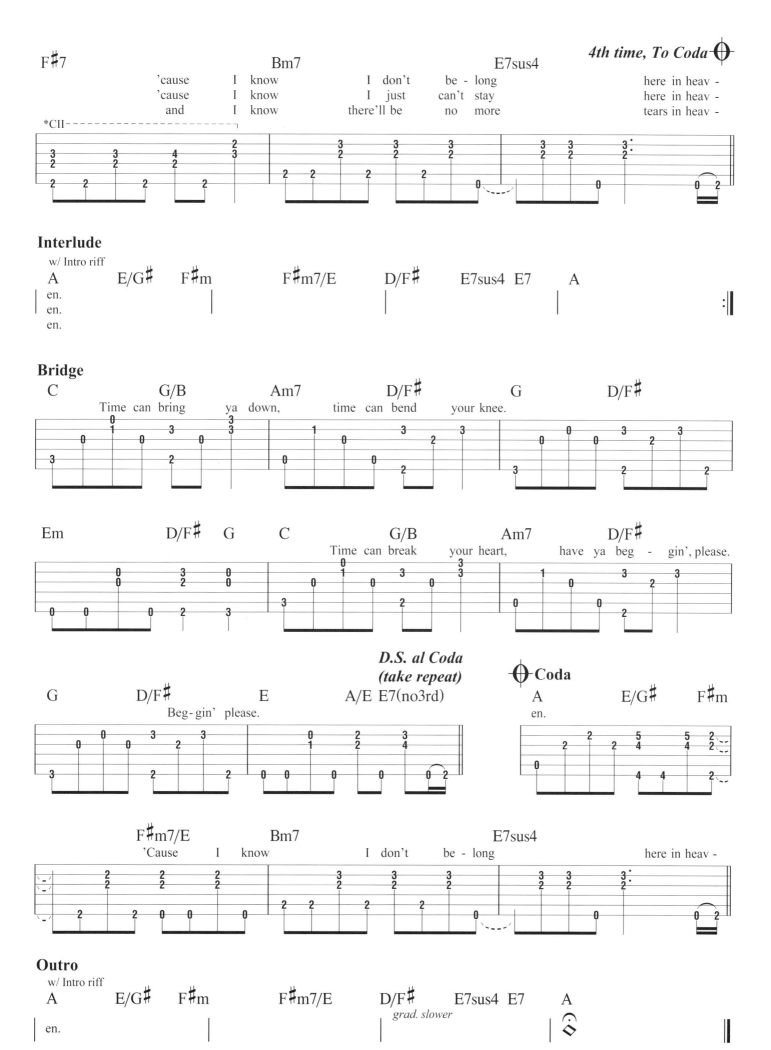

Time in a Bottle

Words and Music by Jim Croce

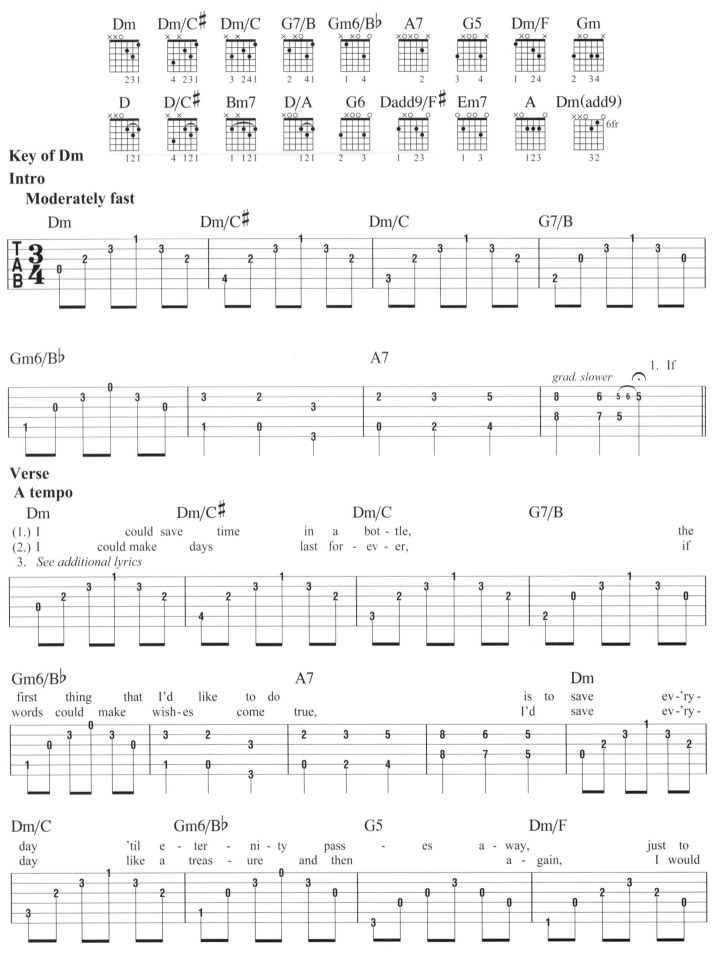

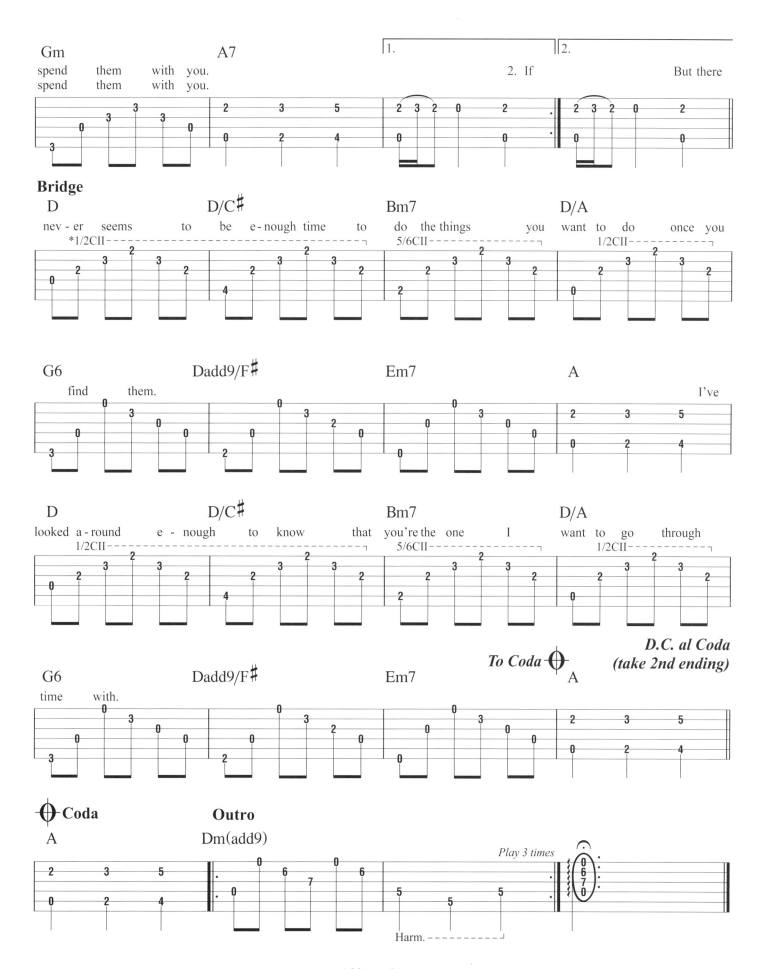

Additional Lyrics

3. If I had a box just for wishes
   And dreams that had never come true,
   The box would be empty except for the mem'ry
   Of how they were answered by you.

*"C" denotes barre. Fractional prefix indicates which strings are barred (e.g. 1/2 = first 3 strings).
 Roman numeral suffix indicates barred fret.

Vincent
(Starry Starry Night)

Words and Music by Don McLean

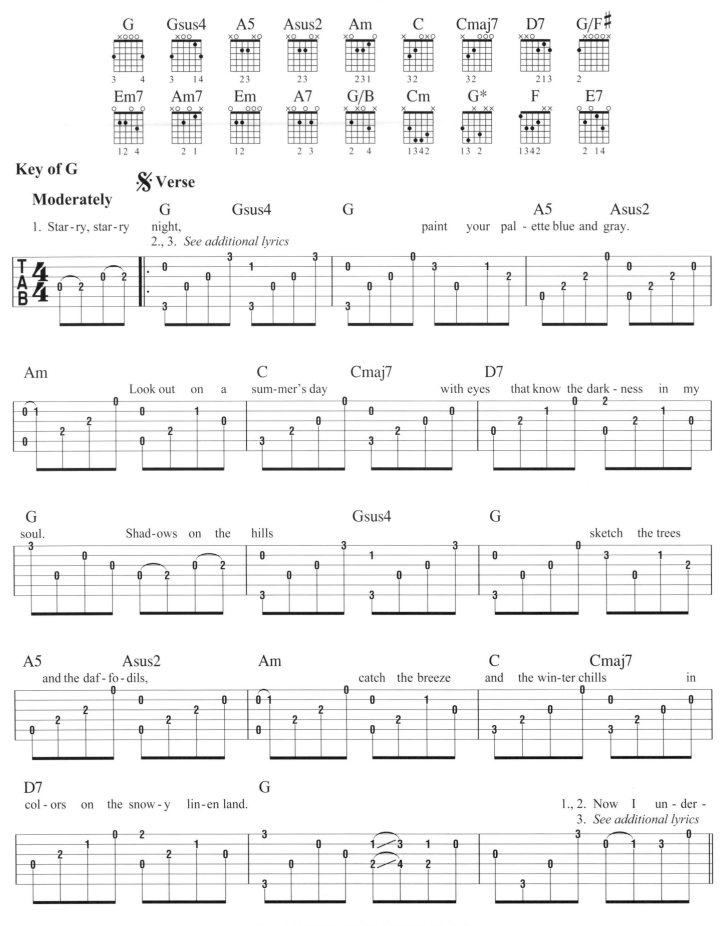

Chorus

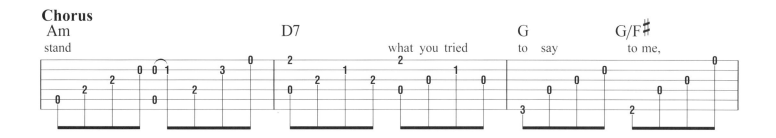

Am — stand

D7 — what you tried — to say — to me,

G — G/F#

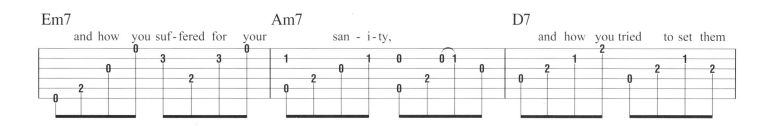

Em7 — and how you suf-fered for your

Am7 — san - i-ty,

D7 — and how you tried to set them

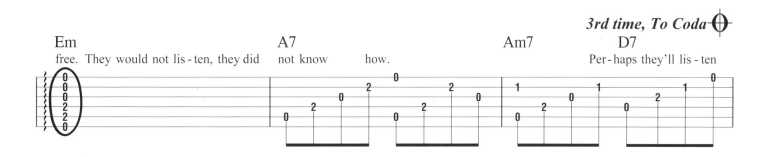

3rd time, To Coda ⊕

Em — free. They would not lis-ten, they did

A7 — not know how.

Am7

D7 — Per-haps they'll lis-ten

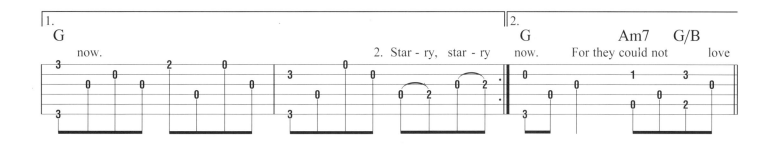

1.

G — now.

2. Star - ry, star - ry now.

2.

G — For they could not

Am7 — G/B — love

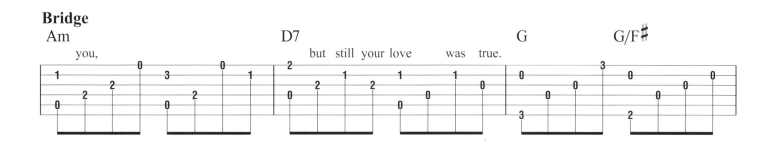

Bridge

Am — you,

D7 — but still your love was true.

G — G/F#

Em — And when no

Am — hope was left in sight on that

Cm — star - ry, star - ry night, you

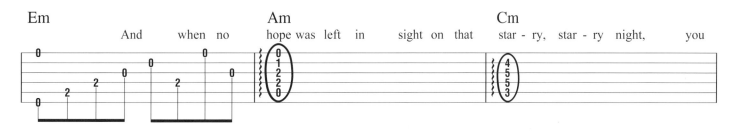

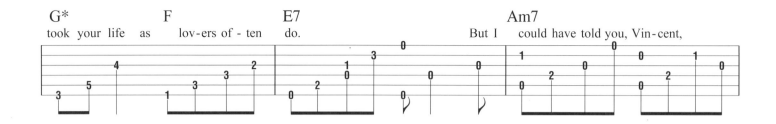

G* took your life as F lov-ers of-ten E7 do. Am7 But I could have told you, Vin-cent,

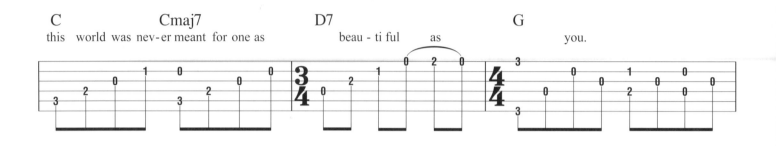

C this world was nev-er meant for one as Cmaj7 D7 beau-ti-ful as G you.

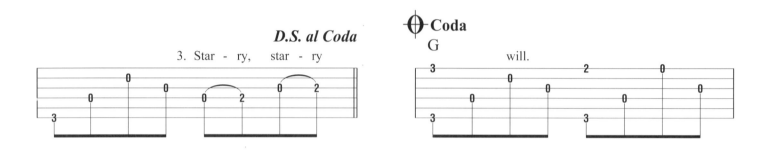

D.S. al Coda

3. Star-ry, star-ry

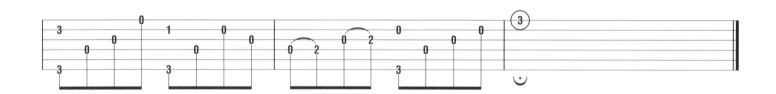

$\oplus$ **Coda**

G will.

Additional Lyrics

2. Starry, starry night, flaming flowers that brightly blaze,
Swirling clouds in violet haze
Reflect in Vincent's eyes of China blue.
Colors changing hue, morning fields of amber gray,
Weathered faces lined in pain
Are soothed beneath the artist's loving hand.

3. Starry, starry night, portraits hung in empty halls,
Frameless heads on nameless walls
With eyes that watch the world and can't forget,
Like the strangers that you've met,
The ragged men in ragged clothes.
A silver thorn, a bloody rose lie crushed and broken
On the virgin snow.

Chorus 3 Now I think I know
What you tried to say to me,
And how you suffered for your sanity,
And how you tried to set them free.
They would not listen, they're not list'ning still.
Perhaps they never will.

When the Children Cry

Words and Music by Mike Tramp and Vito Bratta

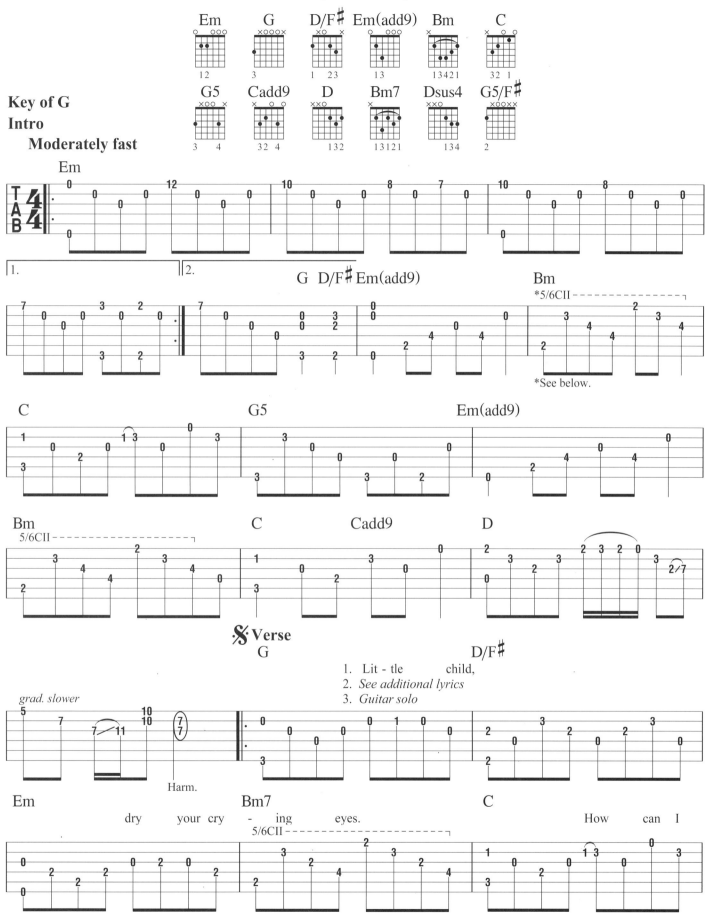

Key of G
Intro
Moderately fast

*"C" denotes barre. Fractional prefix indicates which strings are barred (e.g. 1/2 = first 3 strings).
   Roman numeral suffix indicates barred fret.

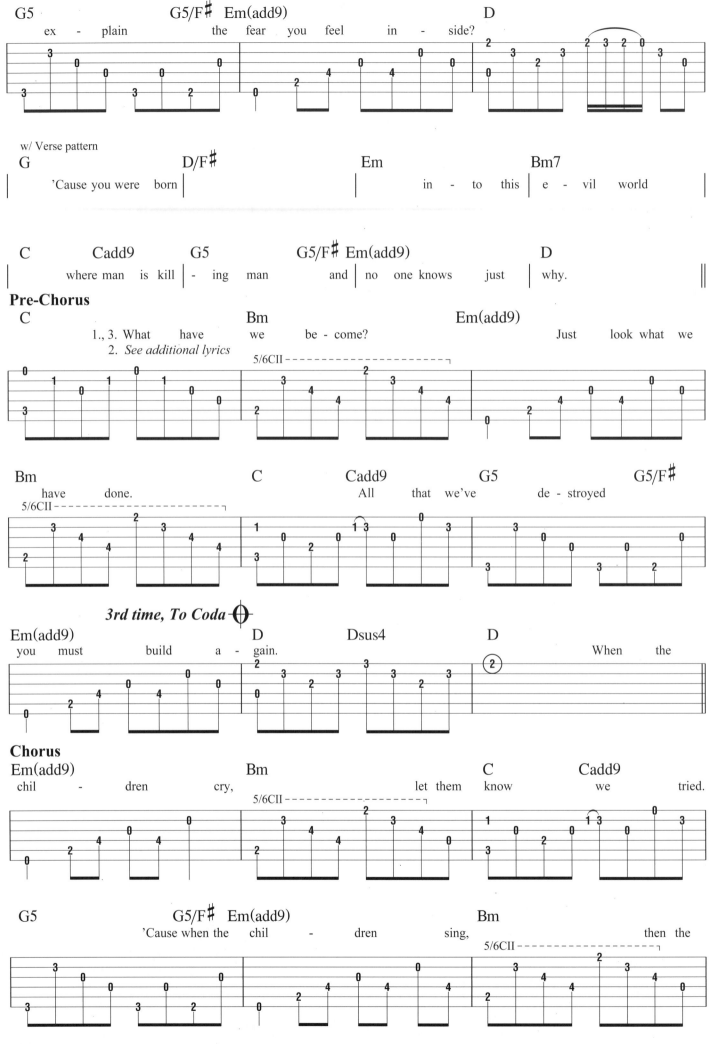

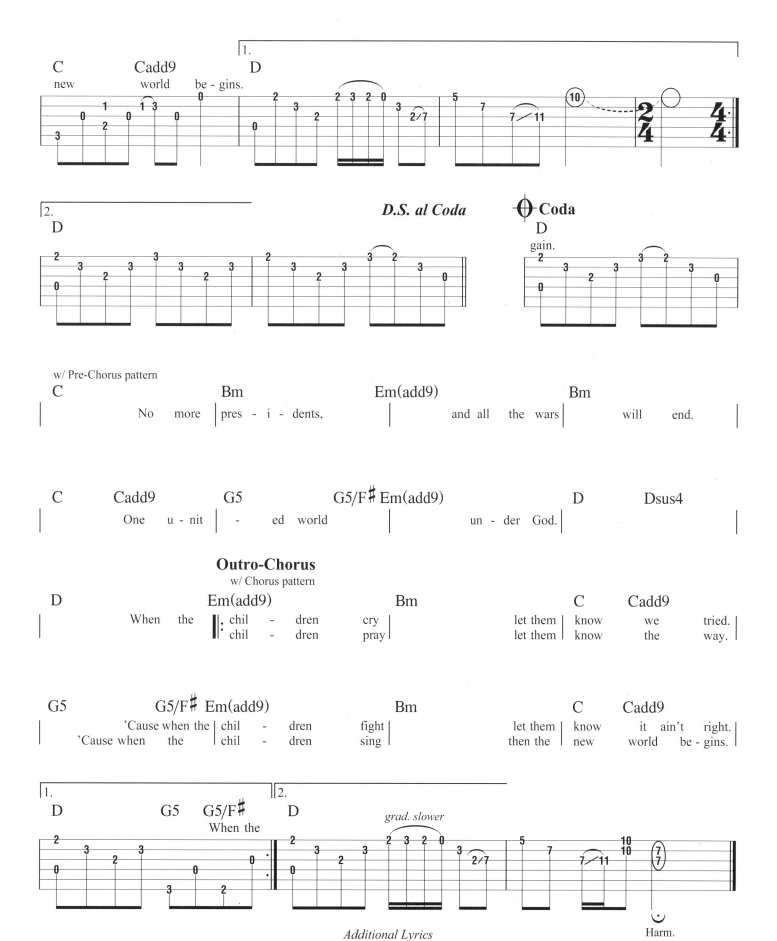

D.S. al Coda

Outro-Chorus

Additional Lyrics

2. Little child, you must show the way
To a better day for all the young.
'Cause you were born for the world to see
That we all can live with love and peace.

Pre-Chorus 2 No more presidents,
And all the wars will end.
One united world under God.

The Wind

Words and Music by Cat Stevens

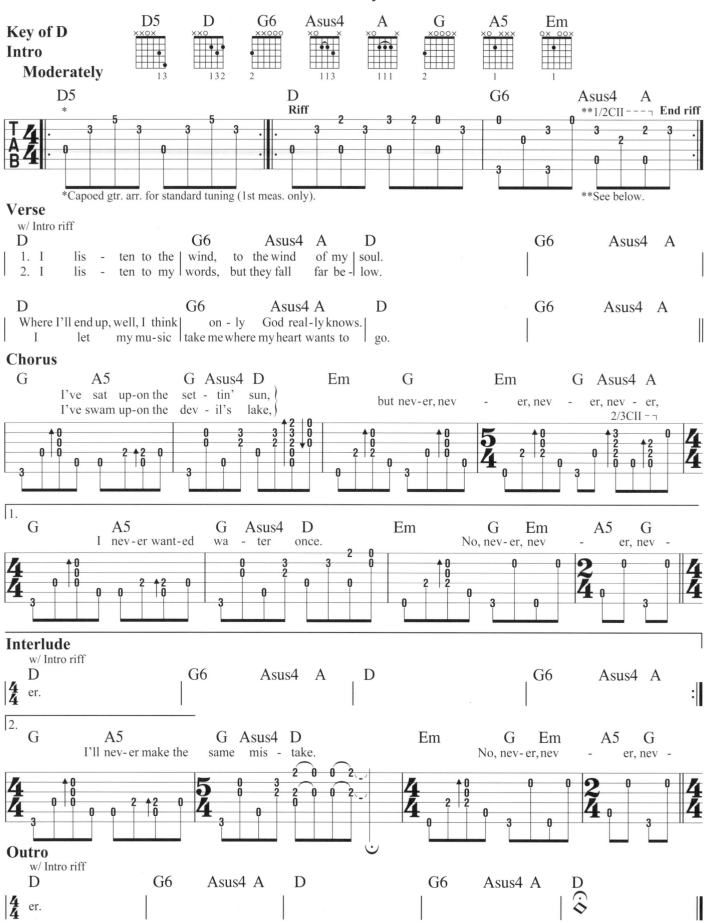

FINGERPICKING GUITAR BOOKS

Hone your fingerpicking skills with these great songbooks featuring solo guitar arrangements in standard notation and tablature. The arrangements in these books are carefully written for intermediate-level guitarists. Each song combines melody and harmony in one superb guitar fingerpicking arrangement. Each book also includes an introduction to basic fingerstyle guitar.

    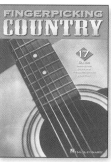 

Fingerpicking Acoustic
00699614 15 songs......................$14.99

Fingerpicking Acoustic Classics
00160211 15 songs......................$16.99

Fingerpicking Acoustic Hits
00160202 15 songs......................$12.99

Fingerpicking Acoustic Rock
00699764 14 songs......................$14.99

Fingerpicking Ballads
00699717 15 songs......................$14.99

Fingerpicking Beatles
00699049 30 songs......................$24.99

Fingerpicking Beethoven
00702390 15 pieces.....................$10.99

Fingerpicking Blues
00701277 15 songs $10.99

Fingerpicking Broadway Favorites
00699843 15 songs......................$9.99

Fingerpicking Broadway Hits
00699838 15 songs......................$7.99

Fingerpicking Campfire
00275964 15 songs......................$12.99

Fingerpicking Celtic Folk
00701148 15 songs......................$10.99

Fingerpicking Children's Songs
00699712 15 songs......................$9.99

Fingerpicking Christian
00701076 15 songs......................$12.99

Fingerpicking Christmas
00699599 20 carols.....................$10.99

Fingerpicking Christmas Classics
00701695 15 songs.....................$7.99

Fingerpicking Christmas Songs
00171333 15 songs......................$10.99

Fingerpicking Classical
00699620 15 pieces.....................$10.99

Fingerpicking Country
00699687 17 songs......................$12.99

Fingerpicking Disney
00699711 15 songs......................$16.99

Fingerpicking Early Jazz Standards
00276565 15 songs $12.99

Fingerpicking Duke Ellington
00699845 15 songs.....................$9.99

Fingerpicking Enya
00701161 15 songs.....................$16.99

Fingerpicking Film Score Music
00160143 15 songs......................$12.99

Fingerpicking Gospel
00701059 15 songs.....................$9.99

Fingerpicking Hit Songs
00160195 15 songs......................$12.99

Fingerpicking Hymns
00699688 15 hymns $12.99

Fingerpicking Irish Songs
00701965 15 songs......................$10.99

Fingerpicking Italian Songs
00159778 15 songs......................$12.99

Fingerpicking Jazz Favorites
00699844 15 songs......................$12.99

Fingerpicking Jazz Standards
00699840 15 songs......................$10.99

Fingerpicking Elton John
00237495 15 songs......................$14.99

Fingerpicking Latin Favorites
00699842 15 songs......................$12.99

Fingerpicking Latin Standards
00699837 15 songs......................$15.99

Fingerpicking Andrew Lloyd Webber
00699839 14 songs......................$16.99

Fingerpicking Love Songs
00699841 15 songs......................$14.99

Fingerpicking Love Standards
00699836 15 songs $9.99

Fingerpicking Lullabyes
00701276 16 songs......................$9.99

Fingerpicking Movie Music
00699919 15 songs......................$14.99

Fingerpicking Mozart
00699794 15 pieces.....................$9.99

Fingerpicking Pop
00699615 15 songs......................$14.99

Fingerpicking Popular Hits
00139079 14 songs......................$12.99

Fingerpicking Praise
00699714 15 songs......................$14.99

Fingerpicking Rock
00699716 15 songs......................$14.99

Fingerpicking Standards
00699613 17 songs......................$14.99

Fingerpicking Wedding
00699637 15 songs......................$10.99

Fingerpicking Worship
00700554 15 songs......................$14.99

Fingerpicking Neil Young – Greatest Hits
00700134 16 songs......................$16.99

Fingerpicking Yuletide
00699654 16 songs......................$12.99

HAL•LEONARD®

Order these and more great publications from your favorite music retailer at
halleonard.com

Prices, contents and availability subject to change without notice.

0122
279

   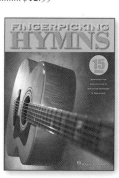  

AUTHENTIC CHORDS • ORIGINAL KEYS • COMPLETE SONGS

The *Strum It* series lets players strum the chords and sing along with their favorite hits. Each song has been selected because it can be played with regular open chords, barre chords, or other moveable chord types. Guitarists can simply play the rhythm, or play and sing along through the entire song. All songs are shown in their original keys complete with chords, strum patterns, melody and lyrics. Wherever possible, the chord voicings from the recorded versions are notated.

THE BEACH BOYS' GREATEST HITS
00699357...$12.95

THE BEATLES FAVORITES
00699249...$15.99

VERY BEST OF JOHNNY CASH
00699514...$14.99

CELTIC GUITAR SONGBOOK
00699265...$12.99

CHRISTMAS SONGS FOR GUITAR
00699247...$10.95

CHRISTMAS SONGS WITH 3 CHORDS
00699487...$9.99

VERY BEST OF ERIC CLAPTON
00699560...$12.95

JIM CROCE – CLASSIC HITS
00699269...$10.95

DISNEY FAVORITES
00699171...$14.99

MELISSA ETHERIDGE GREATEST HITS
00699518...$12.99

FAVORITE SONGS WITH 3 CHORDS
00699112...$10.99

FAVORITE SONGS WITH 4 CHORDS
00699270...$8.95

FIRESIDE SING-ALONG
00699273...$12.99

FOLK FAVORITES
00699517...$8.95

THE GUITAR STRUMMERS' ROCK SONGBOOK
00701678...$14.99

BEST OF WOODY GUTHRIE
00699496...$12.95

JOHN HIATT COLLECTION
00699398...$17.99

THE VERY BEST OF BOB MARLEY
00699524...$14.99

A MERRY CHRISTMAS SONGBOOK
00699211...$10.99

MORE FAVORITE SONGS WITH 3 CHORDS
00699532...$9.99

THE VERY BEST OF TOM PETTY
00699336...$15.99

BEST OF GEORGE STRAIT
00699235...$16.99

TAYLOR SWIFT FOR ACOUSTIC GUITAR
00109717...$16.99

BEST OF HANK WILLIAMS JR.
00699224...$16.99

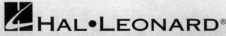

Visit Hal Leonard online at
www.halleonard.com